EMPATHY & ARROGANCE

Dear Miriam,

Its here — finally! Thank you
for the support. I do hope
you enjoy the read.

Your book is on its way to
India, as I write. My
daughter saw it on my nightstand
& grabbed it for a read on the
flight. I will have to wait to
read it :)

Hope all is well. Gurmeet

EMPATHY & ARROGANCE

THE PARADOX OF DIGITAL PRODUCTS

GURMEET KAUR

NEW DEGREE PRESS

EMPATHY & ARROGANCE
The Paradox of Digital Products

ISBN   978-1-63730-686-4   *Paperback*

          978-1-63730-776-2   *Kindle Ebook*

          979-8-88504-030-3   *Ebook*

Dedicated to product builders who persevere while continuing to acknowledge and learn what they do not know about the customer and the problem.

Contents

The Case for Empathy & Arrogance

———

This book is for everyone who dreams of building products that turn our customers into our biggest brand fans. If you are obsessed with your customer experience and can mentally walk the customer journey identifying all the opportunities to make it just right for them, this book is for you. If you are a student or a newbie to digital and curious about the magic of digital, then I invite you to read along as well. I was once a student, and it was this magic and the promise of learning and mastering the art and science of computer programming that brought me to the United States. As I look back, I do not recollect being nervous, although I was leaving my home and family in India far behind. I was rather excited at the prospect of starting a new chapter of my life and pursuing a second graduate degree in Computer Science.

Now, with nearly a quarter-century of experience behind me, I have had many opportunities to learn and build digital products from several different lenses. My career started as a programmer and later morphed into an application architect, where I designed the technical architecture of digital products. The journey continued to meander, and along the way, I learned the skills of both project and product management. I leaned into the power of data and served as the data democratizer ensuring teams had access to the most accurate data and coached product teams on how to use the data to improve their products. Somewhere the path curved, and I led as a digital strategist. In my most recent adventure, I work with a team of product designers.

Each experience has taught me to look hard and deep into the practice of building products. When I first arrived in the United States, the young, nascent me thought strong, sticky, digital products were built on technology. However, the older, mature me has learned from experience that digital products are more than technology. Digital products are about people, our customers, and these products solve human problems. I have also learned that digital products are built with the divergent yet complementary and interconnected forces of empathy and arrogance. As I say this, I pause. Because while empathy is perceived as warm, fuzzy, and deep, arrogance is seen as cold, hard, and shallow. We, as a society, do not want to be associated with any manner of arrogance.

THE YIN AND YANG OF EMPATHY AND ARROGANCE

Since I first landed in the US, technology has moved faster than ever. The world has evolved, leaving behind those who could not keep up. In a very short time, we have gone from the first smartphone connected with a 3G network in 2000, to the first iPhone in 2007—the first mobile device that offered a full version of the internet. Fast forward now to 2021, when there are more mobile device connections as compared to humans on this planet (Tocci 2021).

Smartphones have further accelerated this digitalization—internet-powered devices have replaced books, cameras, scanners, planners, rotary phones. We have voice-activated devices that act as our assistants, self-driving cars, streaming apps, and services with movies and music at our fingertips. But when you think of this rapidly evolving digital landscape, I am forced to ponder: Who asked for virtual personal assistants or apps that monitor everything from our sleep patterns to steps we walk or calories we consume? Who asked to be able to jump in a stranger's car for a ride? And, on a more important note, how did these arrogant product teams build these unwanted and unasked-for digital products and yet get us hooked on them? Did they know more about the customer's needs than the customers themselves? Were these teams obnoxiously confident in their ability to solve these unseen and unheard-of customer needs? Seen from a common person's lens, they appear to be arrogant.

We are living in an era of digital Darwinism where consumer behavior is changing so rapidly as a result of society and technology change that some companies have trouble adapting (Solis 2011). A 2018 study by the growth strategy consulting firm Innosight shows that since 2000, 52 percent of companies in the Fortune 500 have either gone bankrupt, been acquired, or ceased to exist, primarily due to digital disruption. Therefore, if we want to survive, we have to continue to surprise and delight our customers.

As digital change makers, some of the problems we see and face are daunting; yet other issues are minor and easily solvable but unseen by the customers themselves, as we as humans adapt and find workarounds to our problems. Successful product teams do not pause lest we be perceived as arrogant. We cannot doubt our capability to solve these ever-changing consumer needs. Successful product teams continue to challenge the norm while leaning into empathy. They work hard to understand the thoughts, experiences, and needs of their customers and the business landscape while also being entirely aware of their blind spots—this is "empathetic arrogance."

When I think of empathetic arrogance, I am reminded of these words from Steve Jobs, "We believe people with passion can change the world ... for the better. Those people, crazy enough to think that they can change the world are the ones that actually do ... Here's to the crazy ones." (Solis 2011). I am on a journey to learn and master this unique mindset of empathetic arrogance that humanizes digital for our customers and improves their quality of life. If you are on a similar quest, I invite you to read on.

THE ARROGANT PRODUCT TEAM

The thought of writing this book first crossed my mind as I sat in a day-long product meeting and listened to a team present their product strategy. I was first approached by this product team to advise and guide them through the process of building and launching a website. In the initial conversation, the team shared that they were struggling with changing customer behavior. Instead of calling the agents to make the purchase, their customers were turning to the internet to research and educate themselves. With customers moving to competitive digital channels and dropping sales, the field sales team realized the business needed to move its sales online. However, to launch their new website, the company required this product team to follow the internal regulated digital product launch process—this is where I came into the picture. As the company's lead digital product strategist, the team approached and signed me up in an advisor capacity.

As I attended this first meeting, I recollect feeling confused and having trouble following along. Upon probing, I learned that the target customer personas or the fictitious characters created by the product team to represent their target users were "borrowed" from another company's research report, as we had a similar target audience—this was the first red flag. Later in the day, I realized the team was further along than they had first shared with me. I had expected this meeting to be a kickoff; instead, this felt like a conversation to bring me up to speed. The team had identified a technology vendor who was in the room with us. As part of their offering, the vendor had an experience template that they had used to design a sample website for us. The vendor pulled up and demonstrated the website. I asked several questions, trying hard not to sound negative or opinionated—although, by now, there were red flags all over. I felt like the outsider fighting for the customer.

Over the next twelve months, my involvement with this digital product team was sporadic. As the advisor, I was pulled in as the team deemed fit. They followed the internal product building process and received design, technical, legal, and brand approvals, at each point implementing what was minimally required for them to launch. They liked that my role as a product advisor checked off a process box, but most of my questions and concerns went unanswered and unaddressed. I quickly realized that my duties were limited to helping them get internal process-related approvals so they could launch. In their minds, I was the newbie—the one who did not understand the business. In my mind, I was the customer advocate.

The product's launch was met with much fanfare. Postlaunch, the team struggled hard to understand the performance metrics. What should they measure? Did they have the correct data? They presented their product performance metrics to the executive team and touted their two sales in the first quarter—both of which were made by the customers calling the agent to make the purchase, not via an online sale.

As I reflect on my experience with this team, I can vividly recall how arrogant they were about their business and customer knowledge. Although they conducted user and market research that I asked for, they did not truly listen to their customers. They were absolutely confident they knew what was best for their customer. The team's arrogance prevented them from seeing, understanding, and acknowledging their blind spots. These blind spots prevented them from engaging with their customer, identifying the gaps in the digital strategies, understanding the "why" behind the process, and building an impactful digital product. I call this "blind arrogance."

Blind arrogance is feeling overconfident in what we know, which prevents us from identifying and acknowledging our blind spots or what we do not know.

This product team suffered from blind arrogance and was doomed from the start; they built an e-commerce site without truly realizing how the product could alleviate their customer's pain points while differentiating the product in a crowded, regulated marketplace. Let's call it *"Product Doomsday."* We will regularly refer back to this product over the course of this book to understand why it failed.

AN ARROGANT, YET EMPATHETIC TEAM

While *Product Doomsday* is an example of a blind, arrogant team, I want to share the story of a second product team. This is the story of Airbnb, the online vacation rental marketplace where you can rent someone's house. A digital product starts with a problem or an opportunity—or, in some cases a mere inconvenience. In a 2015 Stanford University Blitzscaling class, Airbnb cofounder and CEO, Brian Chesky, shared the Airbnb story was clearly one born out of an inconvenience. (Greylock 2015).

In 2007, Brian and his friend Joe Gabbia—both designers by trade—moved to San Francisco. Brian had $1,000 in his bank account and, on arrival, learned that the rent was $1,150. With obviously insufficient funds to make rent, he and Joe got creative. An international design conference was coming to San Francisco, and upon checking the conference website, they noticed that every hotel listed was sold out. They had an idea: "Designers need a place to stay. Let's create a designer bed and breakfast for the conference." Unfortunately, they had just moved to San Francisco and had no beds; but Joe had gone camping and had three air mattresses. They inflated the air beds and hosted three people from around the world: a thirty-five-year-old woman from Boston, a forty-five-year-old father from Utah, and a thirty-year-old man from India. Thus was born the Air Bed and Breakfast.

These people came as strangers and left as friends. Over the years, Brian attended the wedding of the guest from India and stayed in touch with the woman from Boston as she moved to San Francisco. They realized they had an idea; you can book someone's home anywhere in the world. As Brian and Joe were designers, they required someone on the technical side to assist with the digital aspect of their venture; thus, they recruited Joe's friend, Nathan Blecharcyzk—a graduate from Harvard Computer Science. The three cofounders set out to test the validity of the idea. Similar to Steve Jobs' iPod design experience of the user always being three clicks from a song, Brian and Joe designed the Airbnb website in such a manner that the customer was always three clicks from a paid booking. They created a homepage for the search bar listings, the home, and that's exactly the product as it is today with reviews, payment system, and customer service. They worked through many iterations to keep the customer on the website to complete the transaction.

But it was a rocky start, and they struggled to get traction and build a steady customer base. As Brian jokes, they launched three times just to get press coverage. By November 2008, they were almost broke.

If we think about the Airbnb team, they were arrogant as well, but in a slightly nuanced way. Merriam Webster, the online dictionary, defines arrogance as *"an attitude of superiority manifested in an overbearing manner or in presumptuous claims or assumptions."* This team presumptuously assumed and claimed they had a problem to solve, a problem that no one else saw or asked them to solve. In fact, it was not even a real problem. Who would want to invite a stranger into their home or yet, be that stranger? And why would someone assume that I want to be either the host or the guest? This team was arrogant; therefore, it makes sense that the product did not resonate with their users.

The pivotal point for the Airbnb team was being accepted into the Y Combinator, an American seed money start-up accelerator founded by Paul Graham. Along with providing these young entrepreneurs the seed funding, the program created a structure for the three founders to move in together and work on their product full time. The critical element in Airbnb's success was Paul Graham's advice: "It is better to have one hundred people that love you than a million customers that just sort of like you." In other words, if you have one hundred people that absolutely love your product, they will tell one hundred people, who in turn may tell one hundred or even ten people, and your product will grow. Deeply passionate product followers are also your most loyal advocates.

At the class held at Stanford University, Brian shared, "There was no way I was going to get a million people if I cannot get my mom or my sister to use Airbnb, but I could definitely find one hundred people."

The trio quickly learned that getting one hundred people to love you was not as easy as they thought. To love someone means to know the person really well. To understand what this person thinks, feels, and wants. And this meant the three founders had to meet the hundred people who were going to love them. And so, during Y Combinator, they literally commuted every week from California to New York, where most of the Airbnb community was based.

Joe and Brian went door to door and actually lived with their hosts. Living the experience gave them first-hand insight into their customer experience. They wrote the first reviews for the host places. They realized that some of the house photos they had listed did not do the locations justice. So, they borrowed a camera from their friends in Brooklyn, and Nick—who was also a photographer—went door-to-door, photographing the residences. By better understanding their users—both the hosts and guests—the company started to turn the corner. By April 2009, they had hundreds of people who loved them. People started booking en-masse. Fast forward to December 2020, Airbnb went public with over four million hosts across a hundred thousand cities and more than eight hundred million stays, as quoted on their website.

When compared to the *Product Doomsday* team, the Airbnb team is different. They are arrogant, no doubt. Overconfident in their belief that everyone wants to rent their house to vacationers, they went ahead to solve a problem that was not even an actual problem to begin with. However, it was the empathetic approach to understand their customers better that helped drive customer engagement. They worked hard to know each and every one of their hundred customers to understand what worked and what did not work about their offering. In addition, they had experienced the service they were providing first-hand to comprehensively immerse themselves within the customer's journey. It was this empathetic arrogant approach that guaranteed the success of the Airbnb team.

Empathetic Arrogance is complete confidence to solve an audacious problem while leaning on customer needs, thoughts, experience,

and data to determine if we have the right knowledge and tools to build the product.

THE NEED FOR EMPATHETIC ARROGANCE

Although I came to the United States with the mindset that a higher technical degree, along with the additive experience of working with the best in the industry, would enhance my understanding of digital products, I learned and grew the most when I least expected it. In 2014, when trying to solve a problem with students and careers, I delved deeper into personality types and career fits and was introduced to Gallup, a global analytics and advice firm that helps leaders and organizations solve their most pressing problems. Gallup's Strengths Coaches help you focus on and effectively manage what you naturally do best by understanding your strengths and weaknesses. After talking to several coaches, I got certified.

When I think back to why I chose Gallup, I now know that it was my fascination with surveys and the data-based approach they utilize that attracted me to the coaching certification; however, I was caught off guard by the impact that my coaching skill set had on my ability to build products. While my skill set as a coach helped me build a stronger relationship with my coaching clients, the skills seeped into my interactions with my product customers. I learned to listen to them and built deeper, empathetic relationships with my customers. The product data and charts started to tell a human story. Holistic knowledge of technology, data, business strategies, and human behavior—combined with my coaching skill set—helped me understand digital products at a different level. I learned to lean on empathic arrogance, especially when working with problems that seemed obscure or impossible to solve at first glance. The arrogance, or what might have looked to bystanders as my *"attitude of superiority,"* kept me focused and provided me the drive to do right by my customers. At the same time, my customers and the qualitative and quantitative product data kept me true to ensure I was aware of my blind spots.

As I look around, I cannot help but observe the digital rush; with customers moving to digital channels, companies are rushing to bridge the gap between their analog business practice(s) and their digital customers. However, similar to *Product Doomsday*, not all digital products are successful. Of the $1.3 trillion spent on digital transformation in 2018, it was estimated that $900 billion went to waste (Tabrizi and Lam 2019). This data is based on a recent survey data of directors, CEOs, and senior executives, where the survey participants shared that digital transformation risk is the number one concern. In simple layman terms, "digital transformation" is an act or process of companies expanding or moving their business to digital channels to meet their customers where they are. But the point where companies and product teams often fail is when they think that digital transformation is all about technology. They suffer from blind arrogance. They are confident in their understanding of their business landscape and strategies and believe that they can merely transfer it all to a website or mobile app, and then their job is done. They equate that one action with having transformed their business to a wholly digital state—they are very much wrong in that assumption.

Blind Arrogance	Empathetic Arrogance
Leads with technology to solve a problem	Leads with knowledge of the customer to understand the problem

LET'S DELVE IN

Digital products, when built right, change our customers' lives for the better and make them our true brand fans. We, who touch and build digital products, are the change-makers. Sometimes we think we have/know it all, when in reality, our assumptions and knowledge may have gaps. My goal in this book is to help you understand the yin and yang of empathy and arrogance when building digital products. In this book, you learn to cultivate stronger relationships with your customers by identifying moments of *blind arrogance* and changing them to *empathetic arrogance.* Lean on this book as a maturity primer to check in and remind yourself to be conscious of your actions.

In this book, I will pull from my experience over more than two decades of building digital products. Along with personal stories and experiences with empathetic arrogance, I will also share advice from digital experts — strategists, researchers, experience designers, developers, application architects, digital marketers, customer service representatives, data analysts, and scientists; as well as ideas from thought leaders. The book includes lessons learned from popular products such as Airbnb, Waze, Zappos, and TikTok. I have also included conversations and lessons learned by digital start-up founders from TripScout, Visual Stager, and Markup Labs.

This book is divided into four parts:

- Part One will focus on the foundational mindset needed to build digital products. We will trace the past to see how product development has transformed over the past two decades, thus necessitating a different approach and mindset.

- Part Two will dive into using empathetic arrogance to understand both the customer and the problem we are trying to solve. We will learn what it means to be empathetically arrogant, how it ties into customer obsession, and how it impacts a product's bottom line. Additionally, we will delve deeper into global products and learn to identify global nuances.

- When we have identified both the problem and the customer, in Part Three, we will then conduct a thorough exploration into leveraging empathetic arrogance and the four components of digital products—marketing, design, technology, and data—to build a product that is right for our customer.

- Part Four will focus on building competitive advantage and how to survive in an economy built upon digital Darwinism.

Over the years, I have often been asked to share the secret of building great products. If you have a similar question, this book is for you. And to my dear colleagues and friends in business strategy, marketing, product management, technology, designers, and researchers—this book is dedicated to all of you for the hard work that you do to bring products to life. I hope you enjoy the book, and more importantly, I hope it helps you transform your approach to building digital products and exponentially grow your true brand fans.

PART I

LAYING THE FOUNDATION

A DIFFERENT STRATEGY AND MINDSET TO BUILD DIGITAL PRODUCTS

As was discussed in the introduction, we are currently in an era of digital Darwinism where technology and consumer behavior are evolving faster than businesses can naturally adapt. The impact of this evolution is directly felt on the performance of the *S&P 500* or stock market index, which measures the overall performance of the stock market.

Diving back into the 2018 study by the growth strategy consulting firm Innosight (briefly touched upon in the introduction) can provide us with a true indication of the severity of the situation. The Innosight study shows that in 1958, corporations listed in the S&P 500 had an average stay of sixty-one years. By 1980, the average stay had declined sharply to twenty-five years. In 2011, the average tenure dropped to eighteen years. The study further states that, since 2000, 52 percent of companies in the Fortune 500 have either gone bankrupt, been acquired, or ceased to exist—mostly as a result of digital disruption. Additionally, they forecast that at the present rate of churn, three-quarters of today's S&P 500 will be replaced by 2027.

To be successful in this Darwinian world, it is important to understand the current digital landscape and how to best approach digital products with a different mindset. In Part I of the book, we will delve into:

- **The past:** Chapter 1 will aid us in gaining an insight into the current digital landscape by taking a peek into the evolution and anatomy of digital products. Understanding the product change trajectory will help us better plan and prepare for the future.

- **The present**: Chapter 2 will evaluate the mindset with which we build products and what is needed to set us up for success.

- **The future**: Expanding upon the foundation of the past and present, we will arrive at Chapter 3, which will help us plan for the future by understanding how to frame the customer problem that our digital products solve.

CHAPTER 1

Digital Darwinism

Connecting to the internet over the phone line? Now, that sounds archaic. However, it has not been that long when we used a dial-up modem to connect to the internet. During my early years of graduate school, I could not use the landline phone once I was connected to the internet. If the phone rang, I would lose my internet connection. Those days feel like yesterday, and indeed, it has not been long. In the twenty-six years since I first arrived in the United States, the digital age has increasingly impacted and changed our day-to-day lives.

THE EARLY BEGINNINGS

When I first arrived in Washington, DC in 1995, the world's first website had launched not too long before; created in 1991 by Sir Tim Berners-Lee, a Swiss Oxford graduate. This website—a static page of text and links—outlined how to create web pages and explained more about hypertext. Another memory that stands out from my early days in the US is the limited use of email as personal computers or PC were not common. Compared to the US, where PCs became more mainstream in the late 1980s and early 1990s, it was only far later when PCs got considered a necessity, rather than a luxury back home in India. Therefore, all communication with my parents was over mail, with expensive biweekly long-distance phone calls sprinkled in. I still remember being homesick and eagerly awaiting each phone call and letter from home.

I have vivid memories of awe over my first PC—my own secondhand PC, that is. I felt like a superwoman with power at my fingertips. A personal computer was a must in this new environment, and I compensated for the cost of my very own desktop computer by studying in the library for hours to avoid spending money on textbooks. A few months later, I received a grant at Bowie State University (BSU)—a small, historically black university in Bowie, Maryland. Along with covering my entire tuition for the master's program, they provided me with a paid research assistant (RA) position to work in the computer science lab and build applications for undergraduate students. The opportunity to work and do research was enticing enough to make me change schools.

As I worked in the computer lab developing applications for students to help them understand various sorting algorithms, the world outside was also working on scoring and sorting algorithms for the web search engine. In 1996, Robin Li developed Rankdex. On the Rankdex website, Li shares that Rankdex was the first search engine that used hyperlinks to measure the quality of websites it was indexing, and it predated the similar PageRank algorithm patent later filed by Google. While Larry Page and Sergey Brin founded Google in 1998, Li later used his Rankdex technology for the Baidu search engine, which he founded and launched in China in 2000.

By the late 1990s, with the release of the customer-friendly operating system Windows 95, the Netscape and Internet Explorer browsers, and Google search, there was a rush for companies to have a digital presence. People were using the internet for their basic search needs. Until now, websites were purely images and content, devoid of any interactive elements that we see now. Users could read the content, and that was it. It was right around when I first arrived that websites started moving away from this static, almost brochure-like, read-only functionality. It was the early days of dynamic or interactive websites; users could now interact and engage with a website for simple queries—digital Darwinism was evolving fast and furiously. Next around the corner was e-commerce—the buying and selling of goods on the internet. Both eBay and Amazon started around 1994 and 1995.

I remember eBay, the first digital marketplace, was set up as an auction site. Sellers could list physical products that buyers bid on to purchase. E-Commerce was picking up, and consumer habits were starting to slowly change. With email, increased web presence, search engine optimization, and e-commerce, digital was one of the new marketing channels picking up speed.

A particular recollection of mine was the widespread panic and fear caused by Y2K (or, known to some, as the "Millennium bug"). As complex computer programs were written well before the 2000s, the engineers used a two-digit code for the year, leaving out the "19." For example, when programming, we used the last two digits of the year (like using "95" instead of displaying it fully as "1995.") As the year 2000 approached, many believed that the systems would not interpret the "00" correctly, therefore causing a major glitch in the systems. Programmers were in high demand, and almost every company was going through their code with a fine-tooth comb to ensure there were no hiccups. In December 1999, I chose not to travel and stayed home. Elsewhere in the US, people were also intentionally not boarding flights on New Year's Eve, out of the concern that glitches in computer programs could occur the second when clocks changed from December 31, 1999, to January 1, 2000, and possibly cause planes to stop operating while still in the air. We withdrew money from the banks, stocked up on food and water, and rang the new year in—the twenty-first century had arrived.

EVOLVING USER BEHAVIOR

When I first arrived in the United States, I brought a Walkman with me, as well as a collection of Hindi songs on cassettes. For those of you who possibly do not know what a Walkman is, it was a small portable cassette player made by Sony, just slightly larger than the size of a cassette. And a cassette (also called a "tape cassette") was a flat, rectangular two-inch by four-inch container made of plastic or lightweight metal that held magnetic tape for audio recording and playback. During my commute to BSU on the metro, I listened to songs on the Walkman. My backpack always had several cassettes, at least one book, and I carried coffee or tea in my thermos. Music, books, and coffee became the mainstays of my commutes. Little did I know that the propagation of the digital Darwinism would disrupt each of these precious items, as well as my behavior as a whole, over the next decade.

While the rest of the world was focused on technology, Apple was thinking about the customer experience. In 1993, while at Apple, Don Norman coined the term "user experience" or "UX" to describe the role his team played when architecting the experience for the customers who were using computers across multiple touchpoints. *How do we make the experience of interacting with the computer more friendly? Not just the computer graphical interface, but from the time you purchase it to when you bring it home, unpack it, install it, and turn it on, to using the applications on the computer.* This trend started the shift from the backend technology focus to also thinking about the front-end experience.

With marketing and commerce moving to a digital landscape, the user experience impacted purchase decisions. Before this shift, you went to a store to make a purchase; you bought the object and then used it. With marketing and commerce moving to a digital landscape, the order of shopping and user experience was reversed, and the user experience began to impact purchase decisions.

1. You start by visiting the company's homepage. If the website is efficiently designed and accessible, you then proceed to browse around. If you are successful, you can navigate and find the page for the product you may be interested in. If the information on the product pages seems relevant to you, then you proceed to the next step.

2. You click *Add to cart*, move through the checkout process, and finally give the company your money.

Thus, on the web, the sequence is user experience first, payment second.

The rise of the internet placed purchasing power into the customers' hands. E-Commerce became not just about the transaction—it was about the experience. This shift of priority put extra pressure on the computer industry to improve the usability of its products. As e-commerce sites started to grow, with more purchasing information available, consumers could compare prices online, get deals and promotional codes for money off, as well as dictate delivery dates. Additionally, consumers had the power to write about their experiences online for others to see. With UX determining the financial success of your company and product, executives started to invest in specialized teams within that department.

I vividly remember Gus, the first usability engineer I met at work in 2001. With a graduate degree in Usability and Information Architecture, Gus brought the much desired skills to partner with me to complete user research and design the layout for a website. Coming from an engineering background and mindset, constructing and centering the creation of websites from the customer's perspective was a new venture for me. Along with backend technology and programming, user experience quickly became a critical part of a digital product. The Nielsen Norman Group, a prominent UX consulting group, co-founded by Don Norman, estimates that from 1983 to 2017, the UX profession grew from about a thousand people to around one million people—a growth factor of a thousand percent.

THE CONCEPT OF DIGITAL PRODUCT MANAGEMENT

This shift in mindset was not limited to how we built or designed websites. With e-commerce, the internet also impacted the way companies marketed products to their consumers. Until the 1990s, product managers relied on traditional marketing and sales channels, such as television ads and retail outlets, to promote their products or brand. As the internet became a more common tool used by companies for advertising and selling in the late 1990s, product managers were forced to reposition their products to compete on the web.

The concept of "product management" was introduced in 1931 at Procter & Gamble by Neil McElroy (Devault 2019) to solve the problem of overlapping marketing and unclear value proposition for Ivory and Crisco, the two early soaps of Procter & Gamble. When managing Camay soap campaigns, McElroy noticed that while the flagship product, Ivory soap, was doing well against competing soaps, his Camay campaign was directly competing with Ivory in the marketplace. McElroy drafted a memo explaining his ideas about how Procter & Gamble brands could be built more effectively. A hallmark of McElroy's plan was that one person should be in charge of each brand, accompanied by a dedicated team that focused on every aspect of promoting only their particular brand. McElroy described how these "Brand Men" were ultimately responsible for owning and defining the brand's value proposition, managing the product, tracking sales, advertising, and promotions. The memo further emphasized that field testing and client interaction were key factors of brand management.

The structure created through this brand-centered approach resulted in decentralized decision-making, almost to the extent that each brand was managed as a discrete business. This approach helped identify a brand's unique value proposition, as well as a market segmentation that enabled the product manager to target discrete consumer groups. From Procter & Gamble's perspective, this meant that Ivory soap and Camay soap would not compete in the same market because different markets were targeted for each brand.

McElroy's plan for brand management was widely copied, and versions of it can be found throughout the global consumer product industries today. The same brand philosophy of creating "Brand Men" for each unique product was followed at Hewlett-Packard, making the product manager the voice of the customer within the company. The book *The Hewlett-Packard Way* credits this policy with sustaining Hewlett-Packard's fifty-year record of unbroken twenty percent year-on-year growth between 1943 and 1993 (Packard, 1995).

With digital continuing to impact user behavior, we now had to ensure the products were positioned for online sales. Thus, came the business desire for product managers to be equipped with an understanding of user experience and technology, along with the marketing fundamentals. After working with Gus and several other user experience designers, my first role as a digital product manager in 2006 introduced me to the marketing side of the house. Digital products continued to evolve, thus necessitating me to keep learning and adapting to the changing digital landscape as well.

DEMOCRATIZATION OF THE INTERNET

If the 1990s were focused on laying the groundwork, the 2000s were focused on growth. Mobile phones started to gain popularity around the mid-1990s; I bought my first one around 1998. The phone was almost the size of the current remote handsets and not exactly convenient to carry. But it joined the Walkman, my books, and the thermos during my travels back and forth from client meetings. Laptops had long replaced our PCs of old at that point. I had two daughters by then, and I was focused on creating new traditions with our small family. Fridays were movie nights, which meant stopping by Blockbuster to pick up a movie, followed by pizza and story time at the local Borders on Saturday morning.

Blackberry, the first smartphone, made its debut around 2003 and came armed with a 3G network. I remember my first red BlackBerry as it made it easier to juggle work and family life. The smartphone's simple design and fully featured keyboard flattened the learning curve and were the features that business professionals particularly favored. The full keyboard made it possible to work outside the office. I could respond to emails, texts, and browse the web. The BlackBerry Messenger (BBM) communication service was also a key component of BlackBerry's success because users had an instant connection to people and, thus, could message back and forth without limits.

The Blackberry was followed by the release of the iPhone in 2007. With the iPhone, Apple eliminated the keyboard, which in the Blackberry took up almost forty percent of the display, and replaced it with a giant, all-encompassing touchscreen. It also came with a two-megapixel camera. At that point in time, with a focus on the business consumer, BlackBerry had big government contracts and business deals that helped drive more consumer adoption. BlackBerry did not view the iPhone as competition as it did not cater to the business market. In a 2019 article for *Business Insider*, Alexandra Appolonia details that the iPhone was both more expensive than the BlackBerry and exclusive to AT&T until 2011, which then forced customers in the US to switch providers if they weren't already with that particular network. These factors further convinced BlackBerry of its market monopoly.

So, for a while, BlackBerry underestimated how quickly Apple was updating the iPhone. Determined to change the behavior of smartphone users, Apple continued to iterate away on the iPhone. There was a new, updated iPhone every year, and other smartphones began to hit shelves. In June 2010, the iPhone 4 hit the market with a new front-facing camera, a Retina display, and 512 MB of Random Access Memory. Then came the iPhone 4S; the camera in the smartphone went from 5 MP to a whopping 8 MP, along with video capabilities and the voice assistant Siri. Soon after the release of the 4S, Apple's phone sales surpassed BlackBerry and never reverted back. While the Blackberry was a gorgeous-looking device when compared to my first mobile phone, the 4S surpassed it with its features—which ultimately convinced me to switch to an iPhone. By then, my Walkman had been shelved in favor of the Apple iPod, an MP3 music player that packed up to 1,000 CD-quality songs into a portable 6.5-ounce design, small enough to fit into a pocket.

Blackberry, smug with blind arrogance, missed out on many features that appealed to consumers, like front and back cameras. BlackBerry was slow to change. It focused on designing what it continued to view as a "great product that just worked" and became so arrogant with its market dominance that its desire to iterate and innovate slowed to a crawl. The first iPhone did not win over the market as consumers were hooked to their mobile device keyboards. But Apple did not give up. With each iteration, Apple leaned heavily on empathetic arrogance and continued to enhance and add new features, to shock and delight its consumers. This determination and drive to innovate ultimately led to BlackBerry's downfall. BlackBerry's global market share began a downward spiral, going from 20 percent in 2009 to less than 5 percent in 2012. By the time BlackBerry finally released its spec-competitive touch-screen phone in 2013, it was just too late. (Appolonia 2019)

Blind Arrogance	Empathetic Arrogance
Slow to change due to the arrogance over having a monopoly on the market.	Continue to iterate on the product to surprise and delight the customer

Smartphones truly democratized the internet for the world—a phenomenon that was especially noticeable in India and China. Per the 2019 Statistica data, China ranked first in the list of countries with the most internet users, with India lagging a close second, and the United States in third place.

In India, mobile internet has been a positive development in the country's digital progress; in 2019, over 73 percent of India's total web traffic was coming from mobile phones.

In January 2019, when discussing his book *India Connected: How the Smartphone is Transforming the World's Largest Democracy,* Ravi Agarwal, the managing editor of *Foreign Policy* and former CNN New Delhi bureau chief shared, "Imagine you live in a small village in rural India. Your annual income is around $1,800. You've never owned (or even used) a computer, the internet, or any of the electronics that are a part of daily life in Western nations. Suddenly, you have access to a smartphone. To most Indians, the smartphone is their first camera, first TV, first video device, first Walkman, and first MP3 player. It may even be their first alarm clock and calculator." I noticed this change first-hand when I visited my parents in India. While India had been slow to the PC market, a critical factor for the sudden spike in mobile internet penetration in India was the increased availability of cheap smartphones since 2010, which had created a fertile ground for digital adoption and literacy.

The smartphone not only changed life in India and China but was also integrated into the daily lives of people worldwide. In her 2010 TED talk, "We Are All Cyborgs Now," Amber Case, a cyber-anthropologist, argues that smartphones have become more than just a device in our pockets but something closer to a digital extension of ourselves: "This is the first time in the entire history of humanity that we've connected in this way. And it's not that machines are taking over. It's that they're helping us to be more human, helping us to connect with each other."

I do not recollect when my parents and I transitioned from bi-weekly to weekly, and now almost daily calls, but smartphones changed our family lives, and I no longer felt I lived on an island away from my family.

CHANGING BUSINESS MODELS

Just when I thought marketing, technology, and user experience were sufficient to build good products, the impact of digital started to hit close to home as it began to disrupt traditional business models. Our Saturday morning story time came to an abrupt end when Borders closed its doors in 2011, after forty years in business. Borders' failure to evolve in the digital landscape led to its extinction.

In the 1990s and early 2000s, Blockbuster was a top-rated movie rental store that offered a wide selection of films, though it focused mainly on new releases. Friday evenings meant walking the aisles of DVD cases with my daughters, deciding what movie they wanted to watch at night. Blockbuster's business model was to exceed the cost of purchased CDs by renting them. At the time, it typically cost around two to five dollars to rent a film, with new releases commanding higher prices than old titles. Each time a customer rented a movie, they agreed to a time and day to return it. Late fees, which comprised an estimated 70 percent of profits, were added to a customer's account if they returned the movie after the prearranged date (Christensen 2012).

In 1997, Netflix emerged with a novel idea: for a fixed monthly fee, they would mail DVDs to one's home. This intriguing, newfound method was more cost-effective for us than the rental per DVD, so we made the switch. Netflix made money when customers did not watch the DVDs that they had ordered, which meant that Netflix did not have to pay return postage or send out the next batch of movies that the customer had already paid the monthly fee to get. It was a very different business model than Borders, and they had yet to turn profitable, which my husband and I argued they never would. Our family was on top of ordering DVDs, and our Friday family movie dates continued. In 2000, Netflix offered themselves to Blockbuster for acquisition, but Blockbuster turned them down.

In a 2012 article for the Harvard Business School website, *How Will You Measure Your Life?*, Clayton Christensen, a Harvard Business School Professor and the founder of disruptive innovation, shares that in 2002, Netflix showed their first profit, which got Blockbuster's investors nervous—there was clearly something of value to what Netflix was doing. Many pressured Blockbuster executives to look more closely at the market. Blockbuster responded to these concerns in a 2002 press release, stating, "Obviously, we pay attention to any way people are getting home entertainment. We always look at all those things [...] We have not seen a business model that is financially viable in the long term in this arena. Online rental services are 'serving a niche market.'"

By this time, Amazon and Google were exploring streaming music and movies. But pursuing a new business model with either a DVD-by-mail or streaming required the current Blockbuster operating model to change significantly, as they would need to shift from its brick-and-mortar approach with retail stores. This required investing and standing up of an entirely new way of functioning that was unknown. This only further encouraged Blockbuster to continue focusing on where it was still earning profit. Eventually, Blockbuster responded to all of its perceived competitive threats with similar models, but it was too late. It eventually tried a DVD-by-mail service, rental kiosks similar to Redbox, and put up its own website for online streaming after acquiring a smaller player in the field, but by then Blockbuster had lost. Just like my beloved Walkman, Borders, BlackBerry, and Blockbuster all joined the dinosaurs.

Our family never looked back, and we were soon streaming movies on Friday night. The excitement of walking through the DVD store and arguing over what to watch was replaced by bickering in front of the television—and eventually, on some Fridays, we all hung out together. Still, everyone watched their preferred movie or series on their laptops, iPads, or iPhones.

THE EVOLUTION OF PRODUCT MANAGEMENT

In a 2011 blog titled *"What exactly is a Product Manager?"* Martin Eriksson defines product management as the intersection between business, technology, and user experience. He states, "Only a product manager would define themselves in a Venn diagram. A good product manager must be experienced in at least one, passionate about all three, and conversant with practitioners in all."

In the past decade, digital products have continued to evolve - websites, apps, wearables, virtual assistants, smart home devices, to name a few. With digital products penetrating our lives, we have more customer behavioral data than ever before. Data has further enabled us to build computer algorithms that automatically improve through experience and the continued implementation of said data, thus enabling artificial intelligence-powered products. With data, we can now track our customer behavior both on and off our digital channels, thus empowering brands to serve their customers on their preferred channels.

In my experience, what makes digital products unique is that the users leave data breadcrumbs to help companies understand how they are using the product. Therefore, in addition to business, design, and technology, today's product managers need to understand data. While the product management role is key, it is equally important for each of these four component teams - business, user experience (UX), technology, and data to understand how the components come together to build a strong product. We delve deeper into each of these components and how they interact with each other in Part III of this book.

As the digital landscape has evolved, product managers have become a key component of product evolution. Today, product managers continue to be the digital brand leaders who work across various levels of zoom. They start with an understanding of how the business and the brand provide value to their customers. Armed with this knowledge, they then move on to identify opportunities to better serve the customers in these relentless evolving times. Finally, they bring teams together across marketing, user experience, technology, and data to build a product that is valuable to both the customer and the company. Digital products can no longer be siloed by disciplines; aspects of technology, design, marketing, or data—do not stand alone. For the product to stick, it is vital for these cross-discipline teams to collaborate and build with one product vision in mind.

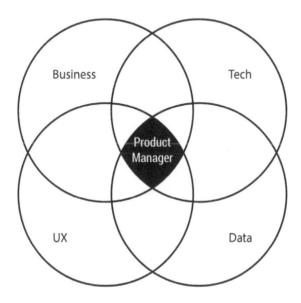

KEY TAKEAWAYS

In a short span of twenty-six years, digital products have become an interlaced component of my everyday life. If you pause for a few minutes and reflect on your use of the digital landscape—for example, think of the digital products you feel you cannot live without—and you may very likely see Amber Case's thoughts resonate with you. Has a product almost become a digital extension of yourself? Upon conducting this exercise on myself, I realized that WhatsApp, the messaging and voice-over-IP service, is akin to a digital extension of myself. I wake up to messages from my friends and family from across the world. It helps me stay connected—and, most of all, I like the video and voice call capabilities that allow me to connect almost instantaneously with anyone across the globe. It has genuinely changed my life as an immigrant. I also discovered that now I leave home with just my cell phone instead of the more traditional physical items that often kept me company in the past. I order my coffee using the Starbucks app, my iPod has been replaced by Spotify, and my Audible and Kindle apps ensure I can access my books on the go.

Digital products continue to evolve from two perspectives: Firstly, the way they are built—starting with technology and growing to impact customer experience, marketing, business models, and now data. Secondly, the speed and sophistication with which they continue to integrate into our daily lives.

Blind arrogance is thinking like Black-Berry, that you have a monopoly in the business market, or like Border assuming that tens of thousands of

book titles in a single store is your competitive advantage, or like Blockbuster's strong belief that your business model is your market barrier.

As the creation of digital products that can compete in the market is relatively easier than brick-and-mortar endeavors, operating within the digital landscape reduces the barrier to entry into new markets. Some examples of the effects of this newfound opportunity for market penetration include the music streaming wars that have emerged between Pandora and Spotify, the power and choice given to the customer via media-streaming services such as Netflix, Amazon, Apple, Discovery, and many others, or even the ongoing competition that exists between ride sharing applications like Lyft and Uber. With the shrinking world, digital products are no longer limited to a particular city, country, or continent— Amazon, Uber, Etsy, Fiverr, TikTok are some of the few products claiming global dominance.

The speed of the digital landscape's growth and spread has been relentless, and there are no signs of it slowing down any time soon. Instead, it has only picked up the pace, and it is a time of what I call *"Digital Wars."* It is back to the Darwinian stages of existence, and this time around, it is a survival of the digitally-fittest. And to win this war, you have to lean on empathetic arrogance. You cannot pause, lest you be seen as arrogant, and you cannot afford to doubt your capabilities in a war. You have to continue to iterate to build a product that solves your customers' needs by leaning into empathy for your customer so that you can see, listen, observe, and understand their changing behavior, wants, and needs. As the digital landscape evolves, the obsession with doing what is right by your customer keeps you evolving, just as Apple continued to iterate on the iPhone to delight and surprise their customer, Netflix continued to iterate on their mailing DVDs business, and Airbnb continued to experience their product firsthand to gain their first one hundred loyal customers.

Blind Arrogance	Empathetic Arrogance
Fixate on the same business model.	Fixate on the changing customer behavior
Slow to change due to the arrogance obtained over having a monopoly on the market.	Continue to iterate on the product to surprise and delight the customer

CHAPTER 2

Playing the
Infinite Game

———

In today's world of digital Darwinism, you can no longer build products by blindly following a process. If you do, you will soon be extinct. In order to persevere and thrive, you need a different mindset and strategy—surviving the "infinite game." In an infinite game, the rules change frequently, appear fuzzy or opaque at times, and are open to interpretation. Competitors come and go, and there is no stopping point to the game. You are either ahead or behind—there is no ultimate winner or loser. The infinite game continues until someone loses the will or resources to keep playing. The infinite game is similar to today's digital world - volatile, uncertain, complex, and ambiguous. In this chapter, we will discuss the infinite game, its guidelines, and how it applies to building digital products.

MY INTRODUCTION TO THE INFINITE GAME

It was 2005; I applied for a web product management role at Earth Networks, a start-up based in Germantown, Maryland. Leading up to this new potential position (besides working as a programmer and application architect), I also had experience leading teams throughout the entire project life cycle. I built applications for federal government agencies and dabbled in launching and running a technical consulting company catering to small businesses, associations, and non-profits. When I first started at WeatherBug, I experienced an uncomfortable, odd feeling—something that I was not used to. In a working environment, I had gotten used to being in control; I knew the process and how to play my role. But this team worked in a different way—one that was unfamiliar to me.

Earth Networks, commonly known as WeatherBug for its popular consumer-facing weather app, was founded as an education partner to schools. They installed professional-grade weather stations at schools and then networked them together. They shared this real-time weather data with schools, broadcast partners, and the general consumer. They were looking for a web product manager with a technical background who had a working knowledge of user experience and business. I applied as I met about 80 percent of the requirements.

Though I had years of experience under my belt, I felt lost at WeatherBug. In all my previous roles, my work duties were defined by a Statement of Work—a document detailing the deliverables and timelines specified by the client—or via a project scope described to me by my manager or the business.

When I worked with clients or even with business teams, I was always clear of what I was expected to deliver, along with the dates and the budget of said delivery. But in my new role, Fran, my manager at WeatherBug, expected me to work with sales, business development, customer service, developers, and designers to first determine what to build and then build it.

Unsure about how to define success in my new role, I observed Fran closely and saw how she participated in brainstorming with much wider teams—including, but not limited to, developers, sales, business development, designers, and testers. I shadowed her and learned how she negotiated what was best for the end customer. I started to mimic her and think outside the box.

Within a few months at WeatherBug, I felt comfortable in my role as the product manager. In partnership with business development, we explored ways to monetize weather data via different distribution channels. One endeavor was an affiliate relationship with Ask.com, a website popular in the early 2000s, which functioned mainly to answer user-submitted questions. In addition to asking questions, users were keen to have access to hourly, daily, weekly weather updates. On Ask.com's website, we displayed updated weather at the current moment; if users wanted additional details, Ask.com redirected them to WeatherBug's website in exchange for a commission. Once users arrived at our website, we provided them with weather data and stories, along with the WeatherBug app, to view weather forecasts on the go. WeatherBug was a serious contender to Weather.com and Accuweather.

Fran and I collaborated with our sales department to create another fun product: weather stickers. Weather stickers were pieces of weather data served up in different formats—such as current weather, three days of weather, weather alert, etc.—all of which adhered to the standard advertisement sizes stipulated by The Interactive Advertising Bureau (IAB). The standard IAB sizes enabled companies to purchase these weather ads based on their customer needs; and, in return for a commission, sent users to WeatherBug's website to get more detailed weather information. The WeatherBug sticker helped drive brand engagement and proved to be a popular and high-performing product.

At all my previous jobs, my work was based on projects with three fixed elements—scope, timeline, and budget. The project ended when the work was delivered. True, when scope changed, we did a change order—yet another document summarizing the changed scope, but it was a very defined piece of work. Whether I was the programmer, the application architect, the team lead, or the business owner, I played by the same fixed elements where I was familiar with the outcome. I had mastered this three-dimensional game and its rules. In hindsight, this was a finite game played with a finite mindset, where the rules were well defined, and the game ended when the project was delivered or, in a few cases, terminated. There was no long-term vision, but just short-term needs to be met. Once the team delivered what the businesses had asked for, our involvement ended.

Blind arrogance is playing a game from win to win with no focus paid on the long-term vision—while arrogantly confident that we are delivering value to our customers.

The game that we played at WeatherBug was a rudimentary form of the infinite game. As the product manager, my overarching objective was to provide current and local, and national weather data to the consumer. Instead of playing a finite game with pre-determined rules and boundaries of scope, time, and budget, I learned to question and determine short term goals: "What is the problem we are trying to solve?"; "Are users getting the weather data they need?"; "Are we able to drive business value?"

It was almost fourteen years later, in 2019, when listening to an Audible version of Simon Sinek's book, *The Infinite Game*, I realized that the team in the Earth Network's office was playing a nascent version of the infinite game. The team was playing small, interrelated games focused on the long-term win. Each game or action helped us move the company and the customer forward. I could see the parallels in the mindset of a product team and playing an infinite game. Similar to the infinite game, when you build digital products, you have to keep the long-term perspective while searching for quick wins—I deem this the "Product Mindset." When you create digital products with this product mindset, it changes the way you build and prioritize features. It brings a deeper meaning to the process of assigning points and allocating efforts to determine the next win.

Empathetic arrogant teams play an infinite game by playing each move with a focus on the future.

Blind Arrogance	Empathetic Arrogance
Focuses on the short-term win.	Focuses on playing small, interrelated games while retaining the vision of the long-term win. Each game or action helps move the company and the customer forward.

WHAT IS AN INFINITE GAME?

The concept of an "infinite game" was first introduced in 1986 by James Carse, the Director of Religious Studies at New York University. In his book, *Finite and Infinite Games*, Carse defines "finite games" as those that function with fixed rules, boundaries, and players. For example, games such as soccer or chess are played with the primary goal of achieving victory. But infinite games are more mysterious— their object is not winning but rather ensuring the continuation of play. He equates friendship, marriage, and even gardens with infinite games. The rules, boundaries, and perhaps even the participants of an infinite game may change, but it continues with the intent to never let it end.

In 2019, Simon Sinek—motivational speaker and author— reintroduced James Carse's idea in his book, *The Infinite Game*, which served as an application of Carse's concept as it applies in today's business world. In it, Sinek shares a story of two education summits that he attended; one was organized by Microsoft, and the second, by Apple. He describes how at the Microsoft summit, about 70 percent of the executives focused on beating Apple. However, at the Apple Summit, all of the executives discussed how to better help students learn, and teachers teach. "One was obsessed with their vision and where they were going; the other was obsessed with beating their competition," explains Sinek. "Guess which one is frustrated in this competition? The finite player is playing against its competitors; the infinite player is playing against themselves."

In his book, Sinek shares his conversation with a senior Apple executive during a shared cab ride after the Apple education summit. He explains how he then informed the executive that Microsoft had given him their latest Zune as a gift after the summit. Zune, introduced by Microsoft in 2006, was a competitor to the Apple iPod unveiled by Steve Jobs in 2001. With a larger body and screen, array of body color options, and three buttons, the new Zune was an excellent piece of technology with a beautiful user interface. Upon hearing Sinek bragging about the brilliance of the Zune, the Apple executive concluded by replying, "I have no doubt."

The Apple executive was unknowingly playing the infinite game. In an infinite game, you will sometimes be ahead and sometimes be behind. The goal is to maintain an eye on your overarching vision and to continue the game—to learn and improve and be better than yesterday, better than the last quarter, better than the last year; to continue to learn and grow or pivot, but continue to play. Despite early sluggish sales figures, as reported by the market research company NPD Group, Microsoft continued to iterate on the original Zune, attempting to compete with Apple, while introducing features like larger capacity, flash memory, and later, an HD touch screen. Though, it could not replace the Apple iPod, which continued to retain its stronghold on the market. Soon, retailers began to drop Zune, with GameStop announcing it would no longer carry Zune, just two short years after its launch.

In a 2008 article on theStreet.com, Priya Ganapati shares this quote from a GameStop spokesperson: "We have decided to exit the Zune category because it just did not have the appeal we had anticipated. It did not fit with our product mix." A few years later, according to a March 2011 Bloomberg article by Dina Bass, Microsoft finally officially pulled Zune off the market. In that same article, a person (who asked to remain anonymous) confirmed that Microsoft would not be producing any new Zune media players; instead, the company would focus solely on the Zune software that already had a foothold on the Xbox 360 and Windows Phone devices.

In this example, Microsoft was playing the finite game with blind arrogance, not really focusing on why it was building the product but focusing on the short-term goal of competing against Apple. This sounds similar to the approach taken by the product Doomsday team, where they wanted to focus on the competition and build a multimillion-dollar product. Apple's iPod changed the way we listened to music and helped grow Apple into one of the biggest companies in the world. Apple continued to iterate and improve on the iPod with the most recent refresh to the iPod Touch in 2019, as per the Apple press release. Apple was playing the infinite game with an empathetic arrogant mindset.

Blind Arrogance	Empathetic Arrogance
Fixates on competition	Fixates on delivering value to the customer

As we continue to investigate and discuss this "Microsoft versus Apple" example, it leads me to question the following: Firstly, how does one differentiate between a process and a mindset? And secondly, how does a mindset become a process, and not the other way around?

MINDSET VERSUS PROCESS

I first "met" Mileha when I came across her TED talk on Inclusive Design held at TEDxDelft in February 2015. Inclusive Design involves developing products, services, or environments with the goal of allowing as many people as possible to easily access and use them. For example, think of entrances to apartment buildings or offices; many have both steps and access ramps for people with walkers, wheelchairs, or even crutches—this enables many people to enter and exit.

Mileha is an Indian-born product designer who traveled to the Netherlands to gain a higher education. In the talk, Mileha recalls fond memories of growing up surrounded by a large extended family. As she recollects playing with her cousins at family events, she speaks affectionately about an uncle who often entertained the children by playing with them. Later in life, that uncle was diagnosed with Parkinson's, a disease that leads to a gradual deterioration of the nervous system. As the disease progressed, her uncle, who was once confident and goofy with the kids, deteriorated in health.

He started to use a walker to prevent falls. The trembling of hands made it hard for him to hold a cup of coffee or tea. Her uncle now hid behind others at family gatherings. He disliked seeing the look of pity in people's eyes.

According to the statistics listed on the website Parkinson.org in March 2021, ten million people worldwide currently live with Parkinson's disease, and the number is growing. Mileha did not want to find a holistic solution for Parkinson's but instead focused on solutions for critical problems that could make her uncle's daily life easier for him to manage. In the TED talk, Mileha said, "As designers, we dream of designing one perfect solution that solves multi-faceted problems. But it does not always have to work like that. You can also solve simple problems and create small solutions and eventually make a big impact."

Mileha's statement denotes an authentic product mindset. How can I add value without trying to solve the big hairy problem? Can I identify small (yet critical) issues that could be addressed to ease the pain rather than holding out to find the big perfect solution to the problem? For this book, I had the opportunity to talk to Mileha; I was especially curious if Mileha was referring to the "Agile" methodology in her TED Talk. In a nutshell, Agile is an iterative approach to building digital products that helps teams deliver value to their customers faster. I was taken aback when Mileha responded, "I was a student in India when working on the problem. I did not know what Agile was at that time." Mileha was not thinking of a process; it was her mindset.

How do we integrate this level of thinking when we build products and be truly agile? A definitive element for achieving it is the act of changing our mindsets to one where we do not merely adopt a methodology at face value. I can teach you the method but, to be truly agile, you will need to think differently. You have to play the infinite game, deliver value to your customer, and outlast your competition. You will need to think of how you can create value faster instead of holding out for the perfect solution. Can you build in small increments, test it in the market, and make changes based on customer feedback? Similar to the Product Doomsday team, when you follow a process without understanding or questioning it, it is your blind arrogance.

When you truly live the mindset behind the process, that magic happens. And you start to live with empathetic arrogance.

Blind Arrogance	Empathetic Arrogance
Holds out for the perfect solution for the big hairy problem.	Provides the customer value by identifying small (yet critical) issues that can be addressed to help ease the customer's pain.
Blindly follows a process without questioning it	Masters the mindset behind the process by learning from, and engaging with, every step of the process.

The first problem that Mileha targeted was her uncle's difficulties with drinking tea and coffee. Once the hand tremors increased, he was embarrassed to drink these items in public. Mileha explored designing a cup that could avoid spillage. By curving the mouth, she created a design that avoided spills by ensuring that the fluid remained in the cup. In her TED talk, Mileha points out that this tool is not labeled as a "Parkinson's cup." Anyone can use it. And this simple device is what makes it easy for Parkinson's patients to blend in. This venture is an excellent example of her passion for inclusive design. In Chapter 4, I will delve deeper into my conversation with Mileha and some strategies that helped her design other products relating to Parkinson's.

GUIDELINES TO DEVELOP THE PRODUCT MINDSET

In his book *Infinite Games*, Sinek highlights five critical guidelines to play for the long-term win. As I think about building products, I recognize that each factor applies equally to digital product teams, too. Each of these guidelines helps product teams focus on how to play an infinite game by making each move with a focus on the future. Let's break down each of these factors to understand how they can apply to us.

EVERY PRODUCT NEEDS A JUST CAUSE OR VISION REPRESENTING AN IDEAL VERSION OF THE FUTURE.

For each product team, it is essential to understand why you exist and what customer problems you are trying to solve. In the stories above, Apple worked on its mission to bring the best user experience to its customers through its innovative hardware, software, and services. This mission kept the iPod teams innovating and iterating without focusing on its competitors. In Mileha's story, she was on a mission to improve the quality of life for Parkinson's patients—especially her uncle. At WeatherBug, we were working to make weather data accessible to people in any format or platform they desired. What is your cause? Do you know why your products exist?

Having a clear understanding of your just cause will ensure you serve your customer and build a product with the ideal future and vision in mind.

EVERY PRODUCT NEEDS COURAGEOUS LEADERSHIP.

In Chapter 1, "Digital Darwinism," I shared the history and evolution of the product manager's role. To ensure product success, digital product managers are responsible for validation, ownership, and definition of the product and its value proposition as the first step. And secondly working with marketing, design, technology, and data to ideate and build the product. Once the product is ready for launch, they work with customer service, communications, and operations teams to launch, and operationalize the product. If the role is played in an unadulterated, true sense, this feat is nothing less than a Herculean task.

Based on my experience, a product manager is the CEO of the product, minus the official authority. While the product manager may not be aware of the company-level details, the product manager has to be mindful of every attribute concerning the product and its marketing. The product manager has to lead by influence as designers, developers, data scientists, marketers, etc., do not report to you. As a product manager, you have to have a passion for solving problems and a mindset to play the infinite game - small wins with an eye on the long-term play. Playing this flexible role with great responsibility and accountability—as well as leading a team that does not report to you—requires courageous leadership. I could not summarize it better than Ken Kellogg, the current Vice President for Digital Commerce, at Mercy Hospital, "Build relationships, everything else you can learn from a book. When you are meeting people, don't talk, just listen. You really start to understand when you're not pushing yourself and your role and your title into things. You just see how things work, and you are able to identify the missing pieces."

Ken's thoughts apply not only to people outside your product team, but also to your team. As you play the true product role, you start to rely on the collective wisdom of the team and the different viewpoints that each team brings when building the product. Create an environment that each team member feels safe sharing their thoughts—this brings me to the next ingredient necessary to play the infinite game: trust.

EVERY EXCEPTIONAL PRODUCT TEAM IS BUILT ON TRUST.
The reason trust is important (or perhaps I would go as far as to say MOST important) is because, generally, when solving problems, the majority of our ideas do not work—and the ideas that do work usually take many iterations to get right. In a 2015 blog post entitled "Product Fail," Marty Cagan, an industry expert with more than twenty years of experience working and training product teams, shares the two inconvenient truths about products. "The first such truth is that at least half of our ideas are just not going to work. There are many reasons for an idea to not work out. The most common is that the customers just aren't as excited about this idea as we are. So they choose not to use it. But sometimes they want to use it, but it's so complicated that it's simply more trouble than it's worth, which yields the same result – the users don't choose to use it. And sometimes the issue is that the customers would love it, but it turns out to be much more involved to build than we thought, and we simply can't afford the time and money to deliver. If that's not bad enough, the second inconvenient truth is that even with the ideas that do prove to be valuable, usable, and feasible, it typically takes several iterations to get the implementation of this idea to the point where it actually delivers the expected business value."

You will fail more often than you win. Just as when Flickr discovered that people loved its photo-sharing feature far more than the online role-playing game that the service had been built for, or how YouTube pivoted after they realized people did not want to look for dates, but instead share content. Having a solid team foundation based on trust is necessary, especially for product teams—so they can permit one another to test, fail fast, learn, and pivot if necessary.

Reflecting on the *Product Doomsday* story that I have shared, no one on the team questioned one another. My questions or voiced concerns were brushed under the rug. If the team had paused to understand my questions or maybe even helped me understand the product goals and bring me along, I could have been an active contributor versus a consultant asked to chime in and get approvals. I lean on Patrick Lencioni, the organization health expert's quote here. In his book, *The Five Dysfunctions of a Team: A Leadership Fable*, Patrick shares, "Great teams do not hold back with one another. They are unafraid to air their dirty laundry. They admit their mistakes, their weaknesses, and their concerns without fear of reprisal."

With trust comes flexibility. When a team trusts one another, we give ourselves permission to play our best game.

EVERY PRODUCT TEAM NEEDS ESSENTIAL FLEXIBILITY.
Speaking at Techcrunch Disrupt in London in 2014, Uri Levine, the cofounder of the navigation application Waze, stated, "Fall in love with the problem, not the solution, and the rest will follow." He urged budding start-ups to know their problem inside and out before even dreaming about tackling a particular market. "If you are persistent at solving the problem, you will become successful," he said.

Uri's words are very much in line with Jeff Bezos, the founder of Amazon, who at a 2016 award ceremony held in Seattle shared, "You want to be stubborn on the vision, and flexible on the details."

In a 2011 blog on this website titled, *Blow Up Your Business before Someone Else Does,* Sinek shared a story about Apple, and it is a perfect example to drive this point home. Steve Jobs and some of his senior executives visited Xerox in the early 1980s to see a new technology they had developed. It was called the "Graphic User Interface," or GUI for short, which empowered users to move the cursor around the screen with a mouse, drag folders, and click on icons. Thus, users did not have to learn a computer language to engage and interact with a PC.

At the time of the visit, Apple was hard at work developing the Lisa—their next major project following the Apple II. They had poured millions of dollars and enormous sweat equity into the Lisa. But when Steve saw the power of GUI to advance Apple's mission to improve the user experience and get the computer into an average person's hands, he saw an opportunity to further his just cause further by leaps and bounds. When they left Xerox, he told his executives that they had to invest in this GUI. In response, one of the executives said, "Steve, we cannot. We have already invested millions of dollars and countless man-hours in something else. If we invest in this, we will blow up our own company."

In response, Jobs said, "Better we blow it up than someone else."

It was this decision that led to the Macintosh, a computer platform so profound that it changed the way we use computers today. This decision also wholly aligned with their mission of delivering the best experience to their customers. Apple has become synonymous with good design, and they have claimed market dominance with this competitive advantage. Are your initiatives aligned to offer your customers value? Do your teams have the flexibility to pivot when they learn their products do not align with the overall mission?

EVERY PRODUCT NEEDS A WORTHY RIVAL.

The mere definition of an infinite game suggests that the game is endless; the objective is not to play to win but rather to continue the game. Sinek defines a "worthy rival" as a company or product that may or may not be in your industry, though it is an entity you respect. Your worthy rivals' strengths reflect your weaknesses. If you are playing the infinite game, you see these weaknesses as opportunities for improvement and growth.

Each product needs a worthy rival, not so you can resent them or try to compete and win against them, but instead so that you can learn about and identify opportunities for growth—ones that are always focused on your product vision. What is your worthy rival doing better than you, which could be seen as an area of potential growth on your behalf? In the Apple and Xerox GUI story above, I almost see them as rivals. Your rival need not be in your field, but it has strengths that you lack. Job's foresight to see Xerox's strength (via their inception of the GUI) as an opportunity for Apple is what propelled the company leaps and bounds ahead of the competition in their game.

In the era of the personal computer, Apple's worthy rival was IBM. As Apple continued to improve its products, IBM's spot in the competition was soon taken by Microsoft. The battle between Mac and Windows was long, but Apple continued to play its cards in a manner that focused on the company's vision. In today's digital landscape, Microsoft's position in this rivalry has been replaced by Google, Amazon, and many others. The competition is now no longer about personal computers but has instead moved on to other priorities, such as data and cloud-based services. All the while, Apple continues to iterate and flourish while remaining focused on its mission to delight customers by bringing the best user experience through its innovative hardware, software, and services.

Many years later, in 2012, when speaking with Todd Bishop from GeekWire, Robbie Bach, the former leader of Microsoft's Home Entertainment and Mobile Business department, gave an interesting post-mortem on the Zune:" The portable music market is gone, and it was already leaving when we started. We just weren't brave enough, honestly, and we ended up chasing Apple with a product that actually wasn't a bad product, but it was still a chasing product, and there wasn't a reason for somebody to say, oh, I have to go out and get that thing." Blindly chasing a rival, instead of taking the time to learn and understand how their product could be innovated to best serve the needs of customers and businesses, is what ultimately led to Zune's failure.

KEY TAKEAWAYS

In chapter one, Digital Darwinism, we explored the shifting and evolving digital world. The internet era has reduced market barriers and enabled companies to experiment, learn and pivot. We are no longer playing a game of business with one opponent; instead, the game board has expanded exponentially with multiple players playing the same game. To build upon the metaphor of a chess game, imagine you are playing multiple games of chess with multiple players, all at the same time. To stand out and to remain in the game, you need a new mindset—the mindset of playing an infinite game.

Blind Arrogance	Empathetic Arrogance
Focuses on the short-term win	Focuses on playing small, interrelated games with one's vision on the long-term win. Each game or move helps move the company and the customer forward
Fixates on competition	Fixates on delivering value to the customer
Holds out for the perfect solution to the big hairy problem	Provides customer value by identifying small (yet critical) issues that can be addressed to ease a customer's pain
Blindly follows a process without questioning it	Masters the mindset behind the process by learning from and engaging with every step of the process

My experience with building products has taught me that you cannot approach building products as a process. Think creatively, as every problem you solve will be different, and it will need a different tool from your tool kit. Keep the long-term perspective while searching for quick wins. Great products are built with courageous leadership and teams equipped with the key elements of purpose, trust, and flexibility to play the infinite game with their worthy rivals. The first step in the game starts with identifying the customer problem you are going to solve. Let's explore this in the next chapter.

CHAPTER 3

Framing the Problem

———

There is a famous example that often comes up when discussing problem-solving: the Elevator Story. Authors Russell L. Ackoff and Daniel Greenberg also share this story in their book, *Turning Learning Right Side Up: Putting Education Back on Track*, first published in 2008. In the story, the tenants of an apartment building were tired of the long wait for elevators. After receiving consistent complaints, the management got the elevator maintenance company in—with their report back being that the elevator was in good working condition with no noticeable flaws. As the apartment management explored the cost and benefits of replacing the elevator, someone suggested, "Why don't we try adding mirrors to the lobby? New, shiny, full-length mirrors to add light and make it a more pleasant place to wait." It would be a relatively cheap addition, so everyone agreed to it.

Once the mirrors were added, the surprising fact was that the number of elevator complaints fell to zero. The solution was not making the elevator faster; it was making the wait time feel shorter. Therefore, the problem, as it was phrased, "The elevators are too slow," is not correct. Instead, the problem is really that the wait time for the elevators felt too long.

Too often, we build digital products that solve the incorrect problem. Before we invest time, money, and resources, let's dig in and understand how to identify and frame the problems worth solving.

JUMPING INTO SOLUTIONS

I fell prey to this same problem in my career. It was 2008-09, right around the economic downturn. I was working with Marriott at that time. The Ritz-Carlton is one of Marriott's luxury brand hotels, and the luxury brand was hurting. Back in the day, with its own website, app, marketing channels, and digital team, The Ritz-Carlton operated very much as an independent brand. This was contrary to the other Marriott brands such as Renaissance, Courtyard, SpringHill Suites, to name a few, which were all sold on Marriott.com. As a guest, if you wanted to stay at a Marriott, you could book a stay at all the brands, except The Ritz-Carlton, on Marriott. com. To book a room at The Ritz-Carlton hotel, you would have to book on the TheRitzCarlton.com website and the corresponding app.

As someone who was well versed in the Marriott e-commerce and Marriott Rewards features, I was tasked with leading the digital renewal of the brand. As we explored options to integrate The Ritz-Carlton website into Marriott.com and eventually sunset The Ritz-Carlton website altogether, I was very confident the solution was to merge The Ritz-Carlton website and app with Marriott.com and Marriott mobile app platforms. The Ritz-Carlton brand could use all the features that were built for the other Marriott hotel brands. In addition to the Marriott website and app traffic, The Ritz-Carlton would benefit from the platform-level investments. It was a technical problem, one that I could handle effectively.

I was really surprised when Kyle, a close colleague, and friend, who led The Ritz-Carlton marketing and digital teams, expressed concern, and pushed back on the approach. Kyle was concerned that my solution fell short of adequately representing the luxury brand. Without adequate brand experience and content, The Ritz-Carlton guests would not understand the value proposition and what really separates the brand from the other Marriott brands, such as the Renaissance or even the Courtyard. Without understanding the brand's value, guests would not be willing to pay for the luxury brand experience, and it would further adversely impact the brand's bottom line.

Despite repeatedly trying to explain how bringing The Ritz-Carlton website over to Marriott.com would actually benefit the brand from having it on the Marriott platform, I just could not understand nor relate to Kyle's concerns. The solution, in my mind, was crystal clear. I had a hard time understanding Kyle's point of view. After multiple meetings with senior leaders, and my unwavering approach, I was excluded from some key meetings, and the project was canceled. The Ritz-Carlton website and app and the team stayed at their offices in Chevy Chase, MD. As I was still at an early stage in my career, I took this as a personal rejection, and it impacted my relationship with Kyle. I avoided him when I saw him in the Marriott corporate offices. I moved on to other initiatives and tried to put what I called "failure" behind me.

Fast forward to 2011, Marriott expanded by acquiring other hotel chains. After purchasing AC Hotels in Spain, Marriott acquired Gaylord Hotels in the US, established Moxy (a new hotel brand in partnership with IKEA in Italy), acquired Delta Hotels in Canada, and Protea Hotels in Africa. After its merger with Starwood Hotels and Resorts, Marriott became the world's biggest hotel chain, with a global presence in 110 countries, 5,700 properties spread across thirty brands (The Hotels & Chain Report 2019). I had the opportunity to lead a majority of the digital acquisitions and work in-depth with the brand teams. As I sat through the conversations— brainstorming about brand value proposition and how the brand stands within the Marriott family of hotels, I learned about branding. I learned to identify the brand's key pillars and worked with digital teams to pull it through the digital experience. Working with brands, I started to understand why I had failed to recognize the objective of The Ritz-Carlton brand integration.

Taking a physical brick-and-mortar business and converting it to operate in the digital landscape does not mean it is a technical integration. You cannot leave the essence of the brand behind when moving to digital channels. You instead have to humanize the digital brand experience and build an experience that lets the guest understand the value of the brand. Many years ago, I had phrased the problem wrong. It was not about The Ritz-Carlton site or platform migration. It was about rebuilding The Ritz-Carlton brand experience on the Marriott platform, preserving the essence of the brand, so guests searching for luxury stays in exclusive hotels can find an option, understand the offering, and book the stay.

I am not the only one who jumped to a solution without truly understanding the problem. In a survey of 106 C-suite executives representing ninety-one private- and public-sector companies from seventeen countries, Thomas Wedell-Wedellsborg, an independent consultant and speaker, found that a full 85 percent agreed their organizations were bad at problem diagnosis, and 87 percent agreed this flaw carried high costs. Fewer than one in ten said they were unaffected by the issue. What they struggle with, it turns out, is not solving problems but figuring out what the problems are.

My experience with The Ritz-Carlton taught me that I was blindly arrogant when I assumed The Ritz-Carlton problem was a technical problem. It was when I listened empathetically to my customers that I learned to identify a problem better. With this new mindset, I assisted The Ritz-Carlton team and Kyle to re-platform The Ritz-Carlton website in 2016. Kyle and I rebuilt our relationship, and we continue to be good friends.

Blind Arrogance	Empathetic Arrogance
Technology is the solution to all problems	Understanding the right problem is the first step in the solution

FADING OF THE KODAK MOMENT

Remember the "Kodak Moment"? The precious moment that warranted preserving with a photograph; the memory that could be relived, again and again, every time we looked at that picture. This tagline was coined by George Eastman, Kodak's iconic founder, in 1892. Founded in 1888, Kodak held a dominant position in photographic film for most of the 20th century.

Kodak was primarily in the film production business. Color film is extraordinarily complex and expensive to manufacture, and this limits the entry of competitors. The sixty-inch "wide rolls" of plastic base material must be coated with twenty-four layers of sophisticated chemicals: photosensitizes, dyes, couplers, and other materials deposited at precise thicknesses while traveling at 300 feet per minute. Wide rolls have to be changed over and spliced continuously in real-time; the coated film is then cut to size and packaged — all in the dark. In a 2011 article for Forbes titled "How Success Killed Eastman Kodak," contributor Peter Cohan states, "Kodak gladly gave away cameras in exchange for getting people hooked on paying to have their photos developed thus yielding Kodak a nice annuity in the form of 80 percent of the market for the chemicals and paper used to develop and print those photos."

With the advent of digital, the world started to shift to digital cameras, reducing the dependency on film. The transition from analog to digital imaging brought several challenges for film production. First, digital imaging was based on a general-purpose semiconductor technology platform that had nothing to do with film manufacturing — it had its own scale and learning curves.

In an article in the *MIT Sloan Management Review*, Willy Shih, the Senior VP of Eastman Kodak Co. from 1997 to 2003, and the president of the company's consumer digital business, shared that when he joined the company in mid-1997, Kodak executives were aware of the digital storm. They continued to track the speed at which digital media was overtaking film, but several factors made it hard for Kodak to pivot and adapt to the new digital world. One of them was that, in contrast to color film, digital imaging is based on a general-purpose semiconductor platform. As a semiconductor platform lent itself to multiple applications and could be easily scaled, suppliers sold the technology to anyone who could pay, thus making it easier for new players to compete in the market. This ease-of-access was different from how the earlier film production business operated, where the complexity of film production hindered other companies from playing in the film production market. Shih states, "Semiconductor technology was well outside of Kodak's core capabilities. Even though the company invested lots of money in the basic research and manufacturing of solid-state semiconductor image sensors and developed some notable inventions, it had little hope of being a competitive volume supplier of image sensor components, and it was difficult for Kodak to offer something distinctive."

In the early 2000s, smartphones with inbuilt cameras infiltrated and monopolized the market, and photograph sharing on social media channels became more popular than traditional printing. As a result of this, digital cameras almost disappeared from the market entirely. In 2001, to bolster its fledgling online business, Eastman Kodak Co. agreed to buy Ofoto, one of the strongest online photography startups. Ofoto offered digital and film processing, online image storing and sharing, editing tools, framing, as well as its own digital photo lab. In a Wall Street Journal article on May 1, Willy Shih shared that Kodak was buying Ofoto because of its 1.2 million registered members and the technology it utilized. The article quoted Mr. Shih as saying that the company intended to merge Ofoto with its online offerings, using Ofoto technology to handle most of the digital printing and electronic-commerce functions, while Kodak will use its technology for scanning and network services.

Despite all efforts, Kodak filed for bankruptcy protection in 2012. It exited legacy businesses, sold off its patents before re-emerging as a sharply smaller company in 2013.

In a 2016 Harvard Business Review article titled "Kodak's Downfall Wasn't About Technology," Scott Anthony, a senior partner of the growth strategy consulting firm Innosight discusses how Kodak's downfall was not about technology. He shares that though Kodak created a digital camera, invested in the technology, and even understood that photos would be shared online. Where they failed was in realizing that online photo sharing *was* the new business, not just a way to expand the printing business. Scott shares, "Before Mark Zuckerberg wrote a line of Facebook's code, Kodak made a prescient purchase, acquiring a photo-sharing site called Ofoto in 2001. It was so close. Imagine if Kodak had truly embraced its historical tagline of 'Share memories, Share life.'"

When addressing the question, "What business are we in today?" Scott suggests that companies and individuals don't answer it with technologies, offerings, or categories but instead think of the problem you solve for your customers. For Kodak, that's the difference between framing itself as a chemical film company versus an imaging company vs. a moment-sharing company. Blind arrogance is framing the mission or objective of your company with the solutions or technical offerings. Because, as we saw in Chapter 1, Digital Darwinism, the solutions will change. If you focus on the solutions, you will lose sight of the mission.

Blind arrogance is framing the mission of your company with solutions or technical offerings.

Empathetic arrogant teams focus on the problems they are solving for their customers instead of the solutions.

Blind Arrogance	Empathetic Arrogance
Defines business with technologies, offerings, or categories	Defines business with the problem(s) solved for the customers

UNDERSTANDING THE PROBLEM(S)

In his 1993 book, *The Five Most Important Questions You Will Ever Ask About Your Organization,* Peter Drucker, the father of modern management, challenged leaders to take a deeper look into the heart of their organizations with five key questions. Almost three decades later, these questions still hold true and are relevant to companies exploring growth in digital channels. In a September 2013 article published on the Inc. website, Peter Economy highlights key elements from Drucker's book. Let's walk through these five questions using the highlights from Economy's article and Southern New Hampshire University (SNHU), a private, nonprofit, accredited university based in Manchester, NH, as an example.

1. What is our Mission?

The mission is the just cause required to play the infinite game. In his book, Drucker says, "The effective mission statement is short and sharply focused. It should fit on a T-shirt. The mission says why you do what you do, not the means by which you do it."

SNHU's mission, as stated on its website, is to transform the lives of learners. They define success by their learners' success, relentlessly challenging the status quo, and providing the best support in higher education.

2. Who is our Customer?

"Many companies are uncertain about who exactly their customers are. And even if they have some idea, they fail to make the customers the focus of their attention. According to Drucker, "Answering the question 'Who is our customer?' provides the basis for determining what customers value, defining your results, and developing the plan." Once you figure out who your customers are, then focus your efforts on satisfying their needs."

In today's digital world, companies have more data on customers than ever before. We now collect an enormous variety and volume of customer information. We have skilled teams to model and manipulate the data to give us more detailed information about our customers.

Yet, in a 2016 *Harvard Business Review* (HBR) article, Clayton M. Christensen, Taddy Hall, Karen Dillon, and David S. Duncan quote a McKinsey poll that found that 94 percent of companies are not satisfied with their organization's innovation results. After decades of watching great companies fail, the authors have concluded that innovation cannot be a hit-or-miss endeavor if the companies are clear on who their customer is. The company's quest to know more and more about customers is taking companies in the wrong direction. By focusing on the trees, companies have lost sight of the forest.

The authors share, "The fundamental problem is, most of the customer data that companies create is structured to show correlations: *This customer looks like that one*, or *68 percent of customers say they prefer version A to version B*. While it's exciting to find patterns in the numbers, they don't mean that one thing actually caused another."

Instead of focusing on the customer, the focus needs to shift on why the customer is using the product or what job is the customer "hiring" the product to do.

Their thought process is that by "hiring" a product to do the work for them, they are "firing" another product or process. So, if online students are "hiring" SNHU to get an online education, they are "firing" other online colleges. Talking to existing customers to understand why they use your product will provide insight into what is sticky about your product and the job your product is doing for your customers.

In the case of SNHU, a customer hires SNHU to get an education. Like many similar academic institutions, at first, SNHU struggled to find a way to distinguish itself and survive. The university's longtime strategy relied on marketing to traditional eighteen-year-old students who had just completed high school and were exploring options to continue their education with undergraduate degrees or certification programs. With no way to distinguish themselves in a crowded marketplace, SNHU's marketing was generic. SNHU had an online distance learning academic program that attracted a steady stream of students. Though the online program was a decade old, it was treated as a side project, and the university had made no significant investments in the program.

If you model the data, both traditional and online students might look similar: an eighteen-year-old and a thirty-eight-year-old working toward the same degree. But Paul LeBlanc, president of SNHU, noticed that the two students were hiring SNHU to do two different jobs. The thirty-eight-year-old is not looking for a residential campus experience and is probably juggling a career, family, and possibly even carrying debt from an earlier college experience. LeBlanc noticed that SNHU's online division had only 16 employees and a few hundred students. He saw an opportunity to evolve SNHU to do a better job for the online customer.

3. What does the Customer Value?

"While this may be the most important of the five questions, Drucker tells us that it is also the one that businesses most often make the wrong assumptions or inferences about the customers' needs, wants, and aspirations. Drucker writes, "The

question 'What do customers value?'—what satisfies their needs, wants, and aspiration—is so complicated that it can only be answered by customers themselves.'""

As SNHU staff met with and interviewed students, they learned that the online students were hiring SNHU to do four jobs: educational credentials, convenience, customer service, and speedy completion.

The SNHU team regrouped and walked through the current online education experience and circled the roadblocks SNHU registration and online education experience were throwing at the students—their customers. Before ramping up and recruiting students to the online program, SNHU needed to streamline enrollment, financial aid, and course sign-up.

Dozens of decisions came out of this new focus. These decisions provided direction on what results to track to ensure they were progressing toward achieving the desired outcomes. They attempted to consider not just the functional dimensions of the job that the students were hiring SNHU to do, such as getting the training needed to advance in a career, but also with the emotional and social ones, such as the pride people feel in earning their degrees.

4. What are our Results?

"Every initiative you undertake will have results, which will need to be collected and reviewed. Results are both a goal and a test that we're on track toward our long-term mission. Drucker shares, "Progress and achievement can be appraised

in qualitative and quantitative terms. These two types of measures are interwoven -- they shed light on one another -- and both are necessary to illuminate in what ways and to what extent lives are being changed." You should make sure you know not just what your results are, but how you can evaluate them."

Based on what was of value to the customers, here are *some* metrics that the SNHU team tracked.

- **Customer service time**: Online students are juggling too many personal balls - family, possibly kids, and careers; they are hiring SNHU to streamline the process. SNHU aims to eliminate the hurdles and replace them with experiences that satisfy the "job" online students need to get done. Therefore, customer service times are essential. The speed with which the team is able to address incoming queries is especially vital to increasing student satisfaction.

- **Enrollment rates**: If customer service is improved and hurdles removed from the student experience spanning across initial interest in SHNU to eventually enrolling in the right program, the team hypothesized that the enrollment numbers would definitely improve.

- **Graduation rate**: The risk for online students not completing the degree is exceptionally high as they have multiple priorities. Focusing on supporting these students increases graduation rates directly.

- **Salary**: Equipped with suitable qualifications and job skills, students should be able to successfully land jobs with market-level compensation.

- **Net Promoter Scores (NPS)**: After improving the SNHU online experience, how likely are these students to refer SNHU to a friend or colleague

5. What is our Plan?

"Given how quickly everything changes today, it's more important to have a plan than ever before. A plan is merely a starting point and not a perfect blueprint. Management must continually refine, adapt and learn, for the plan to work."

Based on the SNHU online student experience, and the metrics the team was trying to move, the team came up with the following plan:

CUSTOMER SERVICE TIMES:
- For most older students, going back to school to continue their education is contingent on financial aid. Time is of the essence, as these students often research options late at night, after a long day, when the kids have finally gone to sleep. Responding to a prospective student's inquiry with a generic email twenty-four hours later would result in a missed opportunity. In the 2016 HBR article, Christensen, Hall, Dillon, and Duncan share that understanding this context, SNHU set an internal goal of a follow-up phone call within eight and a half minutes. The swift response makes prospective students much more likely to choose

SNHU. When prospective applicants place a call or send an email inquiry through SNHU's website, one of its 300 admissions counselors responds in less than five minutes.

- Decisions about a prospect's financial aid package and how much previous college courses would count toward an SNHU degree are resolved within days instead of weeks or months.

- At traditional schools, applicants are required to track down their own transcripts. SNHU took care of this "job" with a turnaround time of two days, at no charge.

GRADUATION RATE:
- SNHU realized that enrolling prospects in their first class was only the beginning of doing the job. To increase the graduation rate, they have to support the student at every touchpoint. In a 2019 Forbes interview with Susan Adams, President LeBlanc shared that once online students are enrolled, they are assigned academic advisers who use Salesforce customer management software to monitor them. If a student falls behind, their adviser steps in, giving advice about how to file for an extension or referring them to SNHU's free online tutoring. This level of support is far more critical to continuing education students than traditional ones because so many obstacles in their everyday lives create additional hurdles for them.

CURRICULUM:

In his interview with Susan, LeBlanc shared that, to design SNHU's courses, he used an approach pioneered by the Open University in England, a mega-school specializing in distance learning. Like OU, SNHU relies on subject matter experts and professional course designers to put together its online courses, which run for eight weeks for SNHU undergrads and ten weeks for graduate students.

THE RESULT

In the 2019 Forbes interview with SNHU President Paul LeBlanc, Susan Adams reports that since LeBlanc took over in 2003, SNHU has gone from a little-known third-rate undergraduate business school with 2,800 students, no endowment, and a budget that was barely in the black, to America's biggest university by enrollment with 97 percent of its students online. SNHU still has a 300-acres campus, dotted with slick new buildings paid for with online revenue. President LeBlanc is projecting a 2020 budget of nearly one billion dollars, a surplus of at least sixty million dollars, and more than 300,000 students by 2025. Let's look at the other performance metrics that have contributed to the overall success of the online program.

- In the Forbes article, Adam reports that as for its six-year completion rate, a measure that's considered important, SNHU's is 48 percent for students pursuing bachelor's degrees. That still puts SNHU a few points below the national average completion rate of 60.8 percent for students pursuing bachelor's degrees, according to government figures. LeBlanc is ambitious and continues to improve the program and says, "I'm proud of our completion rate, and I also want it to get much better."

- SNHU recently paid for its own survey that found its online alumni were earning an average of $51,000 within twelve months of graduation. Adam reports, by comparison, graduates of the University of New Hampshire's main campus in Durham earn a median of $51,400.

- HBR article says that SNHU's online programs have tremendously high Net Promoter Scores (9.6 out of 10) and a graduation rate topping that of virtually every community college as well as higher than that of costlier, for-profit rivals.

If you notice in a bit more detail, the first four of Peter Drucker's questions are focused on understanding the problem, while only the fifth focuses on a solution.

Empathetic arrogant teams understand their customers, their needs and wants, and the problems they are trying to solve before delving into planning.

Blind arrogance is when product teams jump to solutions and build products without understanding their mission, the customer, what the customer values, or how to define and measure success.

My experience with the *Product Doomsday* team was very similar to this. They jumped to a solution without understanding who the customer is, the customer problems they were trying to solve, or how they defined success. Instead, they concentrated solely on digitizing their business model.

Blind Arrogance	Empathetic Arrogance
Jumping to solution without grounding yourself in the knowledge of the customer	Ground yourself with the knowledge of the customer, understand what customer problem your product solves before jumping into solution

KEY TAKEAWAYS

The Kodak team failed to ground themselves on their mission, creating "Kodak memories," and instead focused on building the capabilities that supported the mission; the mission became secondary, and the capabilities became key. In the personal story I shared above, for The Ritz-Carlton, I focused on the technology solution instead of the problem. As we wrap up this chapter, I want you to take away two key points:

1. The organization's mission is its north star. The value that the organization's product creates for our customers drives their engagement and, ultimately, creates value and strategic direction for the organization. The more time we spend understanding the customer problem that our products solve, the higher the chances of success in meeting our goals.

2. In an interview with *BusinessWeek* in 1998, when talking to correspondent Andy Reinhardt, Steve Jobs said, "A lot of times, people don't know what they want until you show it to them." Henry Ford alluded to the same theme in the statement, "If I had asked people what they wanted,

they would have said faster horses." (Vlaskovits 2011). The fact that we think we know more than the customer or that we are telling a customer we are going to give you what we think you need can be seen as arrogance. The key here is to understand our customers' problems. To survive and grow, instead of only focusing on asking what customers need, we need to obsess about our customers, understand their problems, frame them, and then solve them. Ask them to validate the solutions. This ability stems from deep empathy—from understanding the customers and their behavior.

Blind Arrogance	Empathetic Arrogance
Believing that technology is the solution to all problems	Understanding the right problem is the first step to finding the right solution
Defines business with technologies, offerings, or categories	Defines business with the problem(s) solved for the customers
Jumping to solution without grounding yourself in the knowledge of the customer	Ground yourself with the knowledge of the customer, understand what customer problem your product solves before jumping into solution

Armed with a better comprehension of the digital landscape, a mindset of how to effectively build digital products, and a greater insight regarding how to frame customer problems, let's move on to the next step. And that centers around learning more about our customers—this is the only way we can truly understand what our customers need and want.

PART II

EMPATHY

THE NEED FOR COMPASSION AND HUMANENESS TO BUILD A DIGITAL PRODUCT

Computers have their own languages, and these languages have logic. Programming is basically teaching a machine to understand commands and take specific actions. At a very detailed level, all the logic in computers is coded in 0s and 1s. If digital products, by their mere definition, are forms of technology that generate, store, and process data, how does compassion come into play when discussing digital products?

Digital products are used by humans—our customers. If we want to win the heart and minds of the customer, our products must touch our customers' emotions. And who can influence the customer better than someone who understands their day-to-day lives and problems? This is where compassion comes in. Even though our products are digital, which by its mere definition means our users are not in direct human contact with the business, we can pull the human touch and feel through our work.

Digital product builders are change-makers. Digital product builders have the power to impact people's lives, but with power comes responsibility: Responsibility to serve with compassion; Responsibility to always put the user first; Responsibility to leave a positive impact, so our customers become our brand fans and advocates.

In this section, we will delve deeper into what genuine empathy means and how empathy transforms our approach to building digital products. Through the three chapters in this section, we will first dive into the need for empathetic arrogance in the age of digital Darwinism. Next, we will explore how true customer obsession informs us on what to build. And last but not least, we will learn how global cultures and lifestyles impact digital products.

CHAPTER 4

Building with Empathetic Arrogance

––––

When my daughter was struggling in college, I became inundated with her text messages during the day and her phone calls at night. As a freshman in college, she had been calling me every night and, sometimes, even during the day, complaining about her roommate every time I answered the phone. I had started to dread these calls.

Around the same time, in the fall of 2018, I attended an executive leadership certification program at Georgetown University in Washington, DC. While conducting a workshop on effective communications, Professor Jeanine Turner asked us to think back to the most recent tough conversation we had experienced— be it work-related or personal. My mind immediately went to the especially rough one I had with my daughter the previous night.

To help us understand the flow of conversation, Professor Turner asked us to draw a line running vertically through the middle of a page— essentially, a two-column layout. She asked us to label the first column "Think/Thoughts" and the second column "Say/Said." She told us to document the conversation in the second column—this was not particularly easy. Though I remember how I felt during the conversation, I could not recollect our words in detail. Our next task was to fill out the first column. What were we thinking as we were having this conversation? So, I went back to my notebook, and here is what my page looked like:

Think/Thoughts	Say/said
	Daughter: "She is awful."
Oh no, not again	Me: "Why? What happened?"
	Daughter: "When I woke up this morning, I heard her talking about me to someone."
Here she goes again. What is it now?	Me: "What was she saying?"
	Daughter: "She was complaining that my alarm rings and I keep hitting snooze. She was saying nasty things about me."

Think/Thoughts	Say/said
That is super annoying. I would be upset as well if I woke up every morning to my roommate's alarm.	Me: "Why don't you try to wake up when your alarm rings?"
	Daughter: "I try. It has been stressful at night, and I am not sleeping well."
Come on, get your act together.	Me: "Try harder."
	Daughter: "I hate it here. I am asking to change my room."
Oh, come on now! You just cannot make excuses.	Me: "You are part of the program that requires you to stay in this building. You cannot move out. You have said there are no vacancies in the building."

As we discussed the exercise, Professor Turner explained that our brains form opinions, influencing our conversation. She asked us to reflect on how our thoughts in column one affected our conversation in column two. *Hmm, really? Not in this case, I thought. I know my daughter well; I birthed her and have raised her for the past eighteen years.* Professor Turner asked if I felt comfortable sharing what I had written. I remember how we all discussed my daughter's example and laughed at the typical college freshman problems, especially when adapting to a new place away from home—this was in October.

These calls and conversations with my daughter continued through to well after Thanksgiving. She constantly called and complained about simple things: "She had her friends over in the room, and they ate my snacks," or, "I have the upper bunk, and she puts all her stuff on my bed," or, "I am not sleeping well. I crawl into the upper bunk early hours of the morning to avoid talking to her." All the while, I was thinking: *Come on, you have to adapt.*

It was early December when I received an email from my daughter; she had forwarded an email from her counselor as an FYI. Her counselor had approved her change of room; or, instead, it could be more apt to say that she had let my daughter continue in the program but accepted her move to a room with a friend across campus. As I read the counselor's email, I realized that my daughter had been getting bullied for months. Her roommate had sent her messages over text asking her to vacate the room. She invited friends over, and they ate her food and vandalized her stuff; and, as a result, her grades had started to suffer. Why had I missed all these signs? I was talking to my daughter multiple times a day, after all.

I thought back to the day when I had discussed my daughter in class. I dug up the notebook with my notes. I saw that she had mentioned she was not sleeping well. But instead of probing, I had told her to try harder. As I scrolled my phone to review the messages we had exchanged, I saw the same pattern. She was trying to tell me what she was experiencing and asking for help—but I told her to get her act together every time. I had failed my daughter.

What hit me harder was the fact that I had assumed I knew my daughter *really well*. I thought that her inability to adapt came as a result of her sloppy sleeping habits. I was arrogant about my understanding of common freshman problems as this was my younger daughter, and I had experienced it all before with my older one. And this prevented me from listening actively. My opinions and my thoughts had prevented me from asking the right questions and truly understanding what was going on. I learned a hard lesson: no degrees, certificates, or jobs can teach you to be a good listener. And true empathy, being able to genuinely understand and share another person's feelings, starts with being a good listener and observer. You have to learn to read between the lines. You have to see the facts and the data in front of you: Falling grades. More frequent calls. Rapid weight loss.

The incident with my daughter led me to this question: How often are we overconfident in our understanding of our customer problems that we do not lean in to truly listen, observe, understand, and empathize with them?

Blind arrogance is overconfidence in our perceived understanding of the customer that

we neglect to listen to and understand their problems.

My experience with the *Product Doomsday* team left me concerned— so much so that I am writing a whole book about it. In the rush to move their operations to the digital channels, the team forged ahead, overconfident in their strengths and strategies. They assumed they knew the customer well and were acutely aware of what the customer wanted. In these times of digital Darwinism, how can we be more aware of the potential gaps in our knowledge?

EMPATHY, BUT NO CONFIDENCE

If we assumed that most product builders are arrogant, overconfident in their knowledge of the customer and technology, and that the only issue facing them is the lack of awareness of their blind spots—we would be wrong. When writing this book, I had an opportunity to talk to Nick. Sharing his story, Nick explained that he repeatedly noticed how some of his friends found relationships and stayed in them; they did not have trouble maintaining the partnership. Then there were others, who found partners or went on a few dates, but the relationships did not stick. He noticed that these particular friends had trouble building and sustaining relationships. Nick wished for a solution, maybe a coaching app, that could help couples build strong, successful relationships.

As an engineer, Nick saw the opportunity for an app powered by a combination of community input and artificial intelligence. Nick built several preliminary versions of the app, but when users did not sign up for the app, he gave up. Nick further shared that he is a serial entrepreneur; he had started and stopped several endeavors. He expressed an interest in a failure-proof checklist that could teach him how to build successful digital products.

Talking to Nick reminded me of a team I had once worked with; let's call them *Team Unsure*. This team had the most comprehensive customer data and was in a position to build a product that could offer their customers immense value, but they were unsure of themselves. Some of the team members said, "What if it is not an actual problem? If it were an actual problem, customers would have mentioned it. Are we trying to solve an obnoxious problem that does not have legs? "

While *Product Doomsday* was an example of an arrogant team, overconfident to a point where they did not see their blind spots, both Nick and *Team Unsure* suffered from low self-esteem instead. They saw the problems, but they were not sure they could build the right product(s) to solve them. Nick backed off when he faced a hurdle, whereas *Team Unsure* refused to act or get started. In his book, *Think Again*, leading organizational psychologist Adam Grant compares confidence to a seesaw. With too much confidence, we tip toward arrogance. With too little, we become timid—sometimes to a point where it hurts our self-esteem. While we may want to keep the confidence seesaw balanced and look for just the right amount of confidence to maintain, Grant cautions that finding this balance is **not** the right approach.

Confidence is a measure of belief in ourselves. *Confidence is not a measure of how much we believe in our methods.* Grant further explains that humility is not a matter of low self-confidence. The word "humility" comes from the Latin "humilitas," which roughly translates to "from the earth"; It is about being grounded, recognizing that we are flawed and fallible. Therefore, the balance that we must look for instead is *being confident in the belief of achieving our goal in the future while maintaining the humility to question if we have the right tools in the present.*

As a StrengthsFinder coach, I find that not everyone believes in themselves; some lack the confidence to even get started. And we need the confidence to start before we can acknowledge our blind spots or evaluate our gaps in knowledge. Some suffer from imposter syndrome, where they doubt their skills and talents. Others do not want to be seen as arrogant, given society's often negative connotation of arrogance. They would rather wait until the customer says they want the product. But, if you are to survive this digital war, timing is of the essence—and you must have a bias toward action. I would prefer to have the team lean toward arrogance, so it propels them into action.

Instead of holding out or getting overwhelmed by the pressure to find the perfect solution to the big hairy problem, start small. Think of playing the infinite game—but with yourself. Because, in this case, your fear to start is your biggest competitor. Think of how you can create value rather than holding out for the perfect solution. Can you build in small increments, test it in the market and make changes based on customer feedback? If you give yourself permission to play a small game that delivers value to your customer, you will outlast your competition.

As you obsess over your customer, take the opportunity to learn more about them, their experiences, and their needs. Establishing this customer empathy will steer the arrogance to be aware of your blind spots. The yin and yang of the two forces—empathy and arrogance—will balance each other out, with arrogance creating a bias toward action and empathy creating a bias toward the customer.

Blind Arrogance	Empathetic Arrogance
Thinking that confidence is a measure of belief in our methods	Thinking that confidence is the belief of achieving our goal in the future while maintaining the humility to question if we have the right tools in the present

BUILDING PRODUCTS WITH EMPATHETIC ARROGANCE

"I must be the craziest and the most arrogant person in the world to think that I'm going to just go and deliver a disruptive product to the Congress of the United States." These were the words used by Joel Rothstein, CEO of Markup Labs, during our conversation to describe his feelings upon first identifying the problem his company could solve.

Joel recalls attending a meeting with members of Congress. Though the meeting was called to discuss emerging technologies, Joel caught wind of a side conversation taking place, where one of the Congress leaders expressed frustration over simple day-to-day functionality in the organization. "If I could just compare two documents, two versions of a piece of legislation, and then open it in Microsoft Word. I would be so happy."

Others joined in with similar dissatisfaction: "I can't conveniently discuss this with other staffers," "I can't get copies of these documents in Microsoft Word," "I'm getting PDF documents, and then I can't edit them." Instead of worrying about emerging technology and talking to his audience about machine learning or artificial intelligence, Joel just listened. As he listened, he realized that the problem was not emerging technology but rather empowering the congressmen to do their daily job.

As he contemplated the issue, Joel recalls feeling arrogant as he realized that anyone could have built a product to compare documents or a voting product. But no one in Congress was saying that they needed it. And no large company with existing government contracts was telling the Congress members they needed new tools to work on the daily tasks and requirements more effectively for themselves, their staff, and the country.

When building the apps, Joel focused on the fact that this audience were not technologists and that most of them were sixty to seventy years old, some even older. He realized that almost everything in the US Congress operates inside of Microsoft Teams. Therefore, instead of focusing on the technology and asking his customers to stop using Microsoft Word or switch to another messaging tool, he focused on enabling them to manage and take care of their documents within existing Microsoft tools. Listening to the congressmen and not focusing on solutions but merely observing the situation from the outside helped Joel frame and solve their most important problem.

In December 2020, for the first time in the history of US democracy, Democrats in the House of Representatives logged into Markup apps on their government-provided iPhones to cast eleven votes over several days for a variety of contested leadership positions (The Washington Post Editorial Board 2020). The congressmen were surprised and delighted to see a channel where they could collaborate. Joel stated, "We did not invent the electric car. All we did was solve a problem for them that nobody else ever bothered to solve for them."

As Joel demonstrated the product to me, he explained that the iPhone app does only one thing: a vote comes up, you press your selection, you hit vote—and that's it. "That's the end of it, that's the beginning, middle, and end of the app. It was a product that nobody asked us for, and we still went ahead and built it," he added.

BIAS TOWARD LISTENING AND OBSERVING

As we discussed above, to identify customer problems, we have to be able to listen, understand, and share the feelings of our customers. But how do you empathize with your customers when their problems are so different from your own problems, or they entail something that you have never experienced?

In Chapter 2, "Playing the Infinite Game," I spoke about Mileha, the inclusive designer based in the Netherlands. In her TED talk, Mileha spoke about designing products for Parkinson's patients. I had the opportunity to talk with Mileha in late December 2020. I was curious to learn how she was able to identify the most pressing problems to solve in a given situation, especially for a big, hairy, audacious problem like Parkinson's. Mileha explained, "I have the mindset of saying, 'I am not here to solve things. I am just here to understand this person's view, understand how they use objects around them, observe where they have struggled so we can identify pain points. If you can stick to observation and not start finding solutions, because that is the next step. Being conscious of this bias toward finding solutions helps you be in the moment and helps identify and frame the problem."

Additionally, Mileha cautioned that sometimes it is hard to identify problems because we, as humans, often adapt to the situations we face and find temporary work-arounds to our problems. For example, Parkinson's patients have trouble opening jars; therefore, they may not close the jars tightly. If you observe Parkinson's patients, you may not realize this unless you ask questions and seek to understand and deeply evaluate.

Mileha had seen her uncle, who was suffering from Parkinson's, move with the support of a walker in small, unsteady motions; turning a corner involved multiple, meticulous steps. In India, apartment buildings—especially in older neighborhoods—rarely have elevators or fancy rails. She wondered how her uncle tackled the steps leading up to his second-level apartment. She decided to go and observe him as he went about this day, especially when negotiating a staircase. Mileha fearfully watched as her uncle aligned his walker at the top of the stairs. She was utterly shocked to see her uncle walk down the steps in a confident, fluid motion. Later, she learned that continuous or non-stop activity helps Parkinson's patients with their movements.

This learning sparked the thought, "If I can create an illusion of a staircase, my uncle may be able to walk more confidently around this house." Mileha created a picture of a three-dimensional staircase and stuck it to the floor—think of it as drawing a staircase on a piece of paper. She tested it with her uncle, and it worked! She created floor stickers for him to walk confidently around his house, supported by the walker. Her uncle walked faster and more confidently on this illusionary sticker staircase. Sometimes, you cannot help but think of solutions, similar to Mileha in this situation. But instead of forging ahead with blind arrogance, remember to be confidently humble. Your solution may not always work—therefore, always go back and test it with your user or customer before building it.

Mileha did not doubt her capabilities to improve her uncle's quality of life. She focused on understanding the daily challenges he faced. When narrowing down the problems to solve, Mileha did not attempt to find an all-encompassing solution to cure Parkinson's. She instead focused on small solutions that could make a significant impact. She tested preliminary solutions with her uncle before improving them, thus helping enhance her uncle's quality of life.

Blind Arrogance	Empathetic Arrogance
Observing the customer on a surface level, with the sole intent of acting upon an obvious solution	Deeply observing the customer with the intent of understanding them and their pain points to a more comprehensive and constructive degree

KEY TAKEAWAYS

The incident with my daughter taught me to be aware of my blind spots. I acknowledged that even if I know someone (or something) really well, I can never know or relate to their experiences a hundred percent. I then leaned on empathy to strengthen my ability to listen, which allowed me to rebuild my trust and relationship with my daughter.

Empathy means understanding and feeling what someone else is experiencing. When I think about some stories captured in this book, such as the ones concerning Nick, *Team Unsure*, Joel, and Mileha, I sometimes think that empathy alone is not enough. Sure, Mileha could see and feel her uncle's daily struggles with Parkinson's. Sitting in that meeting, Joel could see the problem clearly. Nick noticed the problem his friends faced with maintaining relationships. Joel acknowledged the feeling of arrogance as it is a problem no one else neither saw nor recognized. But he leaned on empathy to learn more about these customers in order to frame and eventually solve the unseen problem. Mileha, too, leaned on empathy to understand the problems experienced by her uncle and confidently built a solution to make life easier for him.

The stories of Mileha, Markup Labs, and Airbnb are all examples of empathetic arrogance. They listened to their customers, and the exasperations that customers felt during day-to-day life. Most of these were problems that customers had adapted to or did not even think of as an issue until they saw a better way to do it. These empathically arrogant problem-solvers observed their customers' frustrations and undeclared needs—and built solutions that helped erase a sizable pain point.

Blind Arrogance	Empathetic Arrogance
We already know the customer	We need to continue to listen to and observe the customer
Confidence is a measure of belief in our methods	Confidence in the belief of achieving our goal in the future while maintaining the humility to question if we have the right tools in the present
We heard what the customer wanted, and we can build it	We understand what the customer asks for, but will continue to validate and test our assumptions as we build

Blind Arrogance	Empathetic Arrogance
We are confident of our strengths and strategies	While confident in our strengths and capabilities, we understand that we may not have the right solution or even address the right problem

As we listen to our customers and begin understanding and identifying their pain points, we get to know them better. We start to obsess over our customers. The more we obsess about them, the better we understand them. In the next chapter, we shall delve deeper into the concept of customer obsession, how it manifests, and how it impacts a business's bottom line.

CHAPTER 5

Obsessed. Maniacal. Radical. WoW

I recently had issues with my cell phone service and had to take my phone to the T-Mobile store. Given the COVID-19 pandemic and the regulation to have limited customers in a store at a time, I decided to book an appointment in advance to avoid the possibility of having to wait outside the store in the freezing December temperatures. When checking the T-Mobile website, I noticed an option to make an online booking, and I managed to successfully schedule an appointment for 5 p.m.

Upon arriving at the store, I learned the team was running behind by a couple of hours and were still tending to the 3 p.m. appointment. I was welcome to wait in my car for the time being, and they would call my cell when the associate was ready to assist me, or I had the option to reschedule. I was frustrated beyond words. This particular store was a thirty-minute drive from home, therefore driving back home and returning to the store was not an option. Juggling the rigmarole of weeknights after work with dinner, kids, and an appointment did not sound appealing, to say the least. Spending two hours waiting in a car did not sound like a fun way to spend a Saturday evening, either. *Why did the website not reflect an accurate appointment count? Did they end up overbooking?*

The associate explained that the website has fixed time slots and does not take into account the number of associates at the store location(s) for a specific day. This misalignment between the website experience and the store experience can easily result in frustrated customers, which means the store employees have to work harder to please them.

Blind arrogance is when we only focus on the customer at a specific point in time instead of thinking through the complete customer journey. As we build digital products, the key point is to remember that the customer experience does not stop at the channel we are building for. Before we launch a digital product or a feature, in this case, booking an appointment on the T-Mobile website, it is our responsibility to make sure we understand how the specific feature impacts customer experience through the entire engagement with the brand. If we want to grow our fan base, we have to obsess over the customer experience with every interaction with the brand. So, how do we define and amplify our customer experience? How can we surprise and delight the customer at every touchpoint with the brand?

CREATING CUSTOMER EXPERIENCE DIFFERENTIATORS

We often associate the term "five stars" with performance ratings for various items: hotel ratings; food ratings; business ratings, clothes ratings—to name a few. Performance for any entity is generally rated on a five-star scale. When interviewed on an episode of the business-centric podcast *Masters of Scale*, Brian Chesky, the CEO of Airbnb, stated, "If you want to build something that's truly viral, you have to create a total mindf**k experience that your customer tells everyone about." And to create a viral experience, Brian suggests we change the question from "*What can I do to make this better?*" to "*What will it take for me to design something that makes you literally tell every single person you've ever encountered?*"

The Airbnb team defined what a five-star experience looks like for one part of their customer journey—in this case, the guest check-in experience at an Airbnb. Following that, they took a step back and went crazy. Here is how Brian defines the methodology:

One star: You get to your Airbnb, and no one's there. You knock on the door. They don't open. If they never show up, you are very upset, and you need to get your money back; that's a one-star experience. You're never using Airbnb again.

Three stars: The hosts don't open; you have to wait twenty minutes.

Five stars: You knock on the door, the host opens the door, they let you in. This is the expected experience, and it is not a big deal. You're not going to tell every friend about it. You might say, "I used Airbnb. It worked."

So, the Airbnb team thought, "What would a six-star experience look like?"

Six stars: You knock on the door, the host opens. "Welcome to my house." The host shows you around. On the table is a welcome gift—possibly a bottle of wine, maybe some candy. You open the fridge. There's water. You go to the bathroom; there are toiletries. The whole thing is great. That's a six-star experience. You would say, "Wow! I love this more than a hotel. I'm definitely going to use Airbnb again. It worked so much better than I expected."

Seven stars: You knock on the door. The host opens. "Welcome. Here's my full kitchen. I know you like surfing. There's a surfboard waiting for you. I've booked lessons for you. It is going to be an amazing experience. By the way, here's my car. You can use my car. And I also want to surprise you. There's this best restaurant in the city of San Francisco. I got you a table there." And you think, "This is way beyond expected."

The team then contemplated what a ten-star stay would require.

Ten stars: Check-in would be similar to the 1964 Beatles' arrival in the US. You get off the plane, and you are greeted by 5,000 high school kids cheering your name with cars welcoming you to the country. As you arrive at the house, there is a press conference for you.

So, what would an **eleven-star** experience be? You show up at the airport; the host is there with Elon Musk, and the host says, "You're going to space."

In the podcast, Brian shares that we know that maybe 9, 10, 11 are not feasible. But, if you go through the crazy exercise and keep going, there is a sweet spot between the customer showing up and the hosts opening the door versus the "I went to space" prospect. You have to go as far as you realistically can toward the extreme end of the scale and then work backward from there. Suddenly, not knowing the guest's preferences and having a surfboard in the house does not seem crazy or unreasonable. It may be kind of crazy logistically, but this exercise creates a great experience. Brian adds, "There's really two stages of a start-up's product. The first is to design a perfect experience; secondly, you scale that experience. That's it."

In a nutshell, customer obsession is going above and beyond what your customer expects; to identify a customer's needs before they can and then catering to said needs as thoroughly as possible. Ensuring that the experience extends across every customer touchpoint (whether they are on the website, app, calling in for support, or at a physical location), and then scaling it to an experience and service that leaves a lasting impression and brings them back to your business, again and again. True user experience goes above and beyond giving customers what they say they want or providing checklist features. This sounds very similar to the approach Apple took when building the iPhone. In chapter one, "Digital Darwinism," we saw how every new iPhone version shocked and surprised the users until it completely monopolized the market.

My T-Mobile experience was a one-star experience. It left me upset and frustrated. The team arrogantly assumed that they had successfully built a feature for the customer to schedule an appointment online and, as a result, likely checked it off their list of priorities—this is blind arrogance in its purest and most straightforward state.

Blind Arrogance	Empathetic Arrogance
What can I do to make this experience better?	What will it take for me to design an experience that makes you literally tell every single person you've ever encountered?

THE CUSTOMER OBSESSION CULTURE

The desire to delight your customer cannot be superficial and thought of only when working on a product. If you do, it becomes a process or methodology and not a mindset - similar to the example of Mileha's mindset and agile practices that we discussed in chapter two, "Playing the Infinite Game."

To be truly customer-centric, it has to be an obsession, so much so that it becomes a default way of thinking.

The Oxford Dictionary defines *"obsession"* as an idea or thought that continually preoccupies a person's mind. When

I think of the term *"Customer Obsession,"* I believe it refers to when thoughts surrounding the customer and their problem constantly pervade your mind. However, Zappos, the American shoe and clothing retailer, describes customer obsession as *"Obsessed. Maniacal. Radical. WoW."* As an article on the company's website entitled "10 things to know about Zappos customer" notes, "At Zappos, you can't escape it. Obsessed. Maniacal. Radical. WoW. Since we first burst upon the e-commerce scene in 1999, Zappos is unwavering in focus on delivering the best possible service experience for our customers. We have always been the first to let you know we are "powered by service.""

In the 2010 Harvard Business Studies article, "How I did it," Zappos's CEO Tony Hsieh talks about his decision to relocate the company. As an online e-commerce company, only 5 percent of Zappos' total sales happen over a phone call. However, Zappos' customer obsession philosophy is to view every one of the thousands of phone calls and e-mails it receives daily as an opportunity to build the very best customer service into the brand. Digging into the data, the company found that, on average, Zappos customers call them at least once during their relationship with the brand. Tony Hsieh believed that if, that one phone call was handled well, they would be able to convert this user to a lifetime customer and that these customers would become strong brand advocates. He strongly believed that the funds that you normally spend on advertising and marketing could instead be invested in customer service.

Obsession with 5 percent of the customer? Most of us would consider a channel bringing in 5 percent of sales not worthy of our time and attention. But it was Hsieh's obsession to deliver an outstanding experience at every single brand touchpoint that made their customers Zappos' true brand fans.

In 2004 the most substantial problem this online shoe retailer faced was how to staff its customer call center with dedicated, high-caliber service representatives. Zappos was based in San Francisco, and the city's high cost of living and the mindset of fast growth prevented folks from seeking a career in customer service. Tony and his team explored options to outsource the call center, but when exploring India or the Philippines, they realized that the differing accents and cultures present within either country prevented Zappos from creating that flawless customer experience they so desired. In the article, Tony writes, "As we thought more about it, we realized that outsourcing the call center would not be matching our actions to our words. If we were serious about building our brand around being the best in customer service, customer service had to be the whole company, not just a single department."

The decision was made to move the company to wherever the warehouse would be located. Call-center employees would be Zappos employees, and the team would be part of the Customer Loyalty Team. After much thought and exploring many options, they decided to move the company to Las Vegas, where hospitality and twenty-four-seven support are part of the city culture. Surprisingly, more than 75 percent of the staff was willing to relocate, and the company culture became even stronger as a result of the move.

On Zappos' website, the company has listed the ten things that make its customer-centric culture so fabulous:

1. Easy-to-find contact info on every single website page, mobile app, and Google search result; you cannot miss it.

2. Unlimited call times with the currently longest call running at ten hours, fifty-one minutes.

3. Friendly, solution-oriented representatives; conversation topics include personal matters, such as weddings, pregnancies, graduations, birthdays, and anniversaries.

4. No phone tree—which means you do not have to dial numbers in circles.

5. No scripts or templates, which means you can have an actual conversation with a human.

6. Twenty-four-seven call centers, so you can call them anytime.

7. Customers have 365 days, a whole year, to return or exchange their purchase.

8. All Customer Loyalty Team members are empowered to help, so there will not be any cases of "let me check with my manager."

9. Free shipping and returns always. And, perhaps most important:

10. No up-selling. When you call, no one will try to sell you a more expensive shoe or a purse.

Based on this list, Zappos truly designs the customer experience the way Brian Chesky explains it. Almost every customer experience touchpoint described on the list goes above and beyond the five-star performance rating. In a 2009 letter to his employees to inform them of Zappos' acquisition by Amazon, Tony shared an eight-minute YouTube video from Jeff Bezos to provide his employees with some insight into Bezos's personality and way of thinking. In the video, Bezos stated it was Zappos' obsession with the customer at every single brand touchpoint that won his heart and made him "weak in the knees".

Blind Arrogance	Empathetic Arrogance
Focusing on the customer at a specific point in time in the customer journey	Obsessing about the customer experience at every point in a customer's interaction with the brand.

CUSTOMER OBSESSION INFORMS WHAT TO BUILD

The capital of the United States, Washington, DC, is famous for its iconic buildings—the Capitol, the White House, the Supreme Court, alongside the monuments and museums that line Constitution Avenue, starting from the Lincoln Memorial stretching all the way to the Capitol. Beginning in April, with the Cherry Blossom blooming around the tidal basin, tourists flock to the city. With performing centers, art museums, and restaurants, hotels, and Airbnbs are booked months in advance. However, in the summer of 2020, the city was deserted. The COVID-19 pandemic had laid the city to waste. Office buildings and museums were closed. With stay-at-home orders in place, the town was deserted. Hotels and restaurants were shuttered. City dwellers left the city in search of open spaces in the suburbs.

My condo in the city, which was usually in high demand, sat vacant for nearly six months. Desperate to get it rented, I called staging companies to explore rates; I hoped staging would help prospective tenants see the small 500 sq ft. unit in a different light. With staging estimates nearing almost $3000, I gave up on the idea. Another month passed by with no luck, and once again, I started to search for a potential cheaper staging option. One day, while searching on the internet, Google results displayed virtual staging companies. I was curious to learn more and started to dig deeper into the option.

I came across VisualStager, a web application that ranked higher than other virtual staging options on Google search results. The following Sunday, I spent the afternoon creating an account, uploading pictures of the empty unit, and dragging and dropping furniture in place. When I ran into a hurdle, I followed instructions and emailed customer service. I got a response to my issue in a couple of hours. I continued to play with different furniture layouts, modern versus traditional furniture, couch against the wall, or separating the big living space into two livable sections; I played around until it felt right. By the end of the afternoon, I had a few pictures to upload on Zillow for my rental listing. I was surprised to see the number of leads these new images generated—and, within eight weeks, I was finally able to rent the unit.

When writing this book, I reached out to Parag Tope, the founder of VisualStager, to learn about his inspiration behind the application. Parag initially came to the United States from Pune, India, to obtain a master's degree in Mechanical Engineering at Clemson University. After pursuing an MBA at Michigan, he worked in the auto industry. An opportunity to work for a start-up brought him to the West Coast, and eventually, in the early 2000s, he started his own services company. He worked with builders, taking new construction floor plans and elevations, and converting them to 3D renders and animations. The company also provided builders with digital services, enabling them to showcase the construction to the city council planning commission to get approvals and market these homes to prospective buyers.

In February 2011, when furnishing the construction property for city walkthrough, Parag was walking through a space when someone thought out loud, "Hey, if I already had a property, and I had photographs, it would be cool to be able to digitally add furniture to the property pictures." Parag knew this was pretty easy to accomplish with three-dimensional modeling software like AutoCAD or similar free alternatives. What enticed him was the idea of a tool that enabled a layperson not versed in three-dimensional software to do it themselves. Wired as a problem solver, Parag spent time thinking about the challenge and came up with a proof of concept (POC) in a month. A POC focuses on a small piece of the overall solution with the goal to evaluate its feasibility and reduce implementation risk. It is used in the early stages when you first have an instinct about an idea.

With a proof of concept in hand, Parag moved on to develop a working prototype. Prototypes are used when you have a hypothesis about a solution, but you are still uncertain about how it will look, feel, and work in a practical capacity. A proof of concept shows if a product or feature *can* be developed, while a prototype shows *how* it will be developed. As Parag had confirmed feasibility with a POC, he built a working prototype to put in front of his prospective customers and get feedback.

In November 2012, with a functioning prototype, Parag attended the National Association of Realtors show in Florida, where he had the opportunity to share and test his prototype with participating realtors. The response to the app was overwhelming and confirmed the need for the product. Armed with insights from the testing, Parag continued to work on it for another six months—and finally, in 2013, VisualStager launched to the public.

Technically, the virtual staging product is pretty complex. But what differentiates VisualStager is that it enables you to add a three-dimensional couch to a two-dimensional photograph. So, you can upload a picture of your room and then drag and drop items from a library of furniture options onto your photograph. The end result is a photograph of a staged room. Voila! This enables it to work on a web browser, and the end result looks very realistic.

While VisualStager collects usage data to gain holistic performance metrics, Parag has intentionally focused on interacting with and learning from his customers. Parag says, "We can collect and dig into additional data to learn where and how we can optimize the product, but instead by working directly with our consumers, we are able to quickly identify the major pain points, fix or build and create the big wins." Through this obsession of ingraining themselves amidst their customers versus analyzing data for customer insights, VisualStager has grown its market share. Their users are engaged and vocal about providing feedback. If something is ambiguous or not working, the product team hears about it. They receive both positive and negative feedback that makes it easier for them to understand the friction points or stumbling blocks.

Over the years after launching it, the VisualStager team made several iterations and changes to the product based on the customer feedback they received. At launch, VisualStager had approximately five hundred items of furniture; the product team thought this was a decent number. But, very early on in the postlaunch phase, the team received enormous amounts of feedback concerning furniture; customers were asking for more. So, each month, the team started to add hundreds of items; today, they are at approximately five thousand pieces of furniture. With this new influx of items came the issue of sorting and filtering to pick furniture that best met customer needs. To help the customer, the team added categorization, filtering, and rating frameworks. The rating model empowered the customer to rate the items and then use the ones they liked. Because users did not want to drown in the vastly expanding furniture library, the product team also added a new feature where customers could import from rooms and furniture items they had created before. Additionally, based on customer needs, the VisualStager team created several hundred pre-designed rooms that enabled customers to browse, pick an item, add it to their room, and move it around.

Parag describes small businesses—such as small and large brokerages, agents, photographers, interior designers, to name a few—as key customers of VisualStager, as they see the immediate value. Users like myself, who are using the product to solve their immediate needs, are few. While there is a largely untapped audience for VisualStager in the commercial business market, Parag is very clear and obsessed with product performance for his target audience; he prefers to focus on keeping his critical, small-business customers happy. These customers, in turn, are his biggest advocates and brand fans. To date, the team has not spent any marketing dollars—great user reviews serve as their advertisements, and happy customers keep coming back to the product.

Blind Arrogance	Empathetic Arrogance
We know what product features improve business value	We know what product features improve the customer's experience while providing business value
Reading customer persona report to understand the customer	Embedding yourself in the customer community to listen to and observe the customer
Focusing on product performance data to identify new features	Identifying new product features by focusing on the customer to recognize their problems and using the data to augment your understanding

CUSTOMER OBSESSION IMPACTS THE BUSINESS BOTTOM LINE

A 2015 research study conducted at one of the top five consulting companies, Bain & Company, found that the companies that focus on customer experience grow faster than their competitor by 4 percent to 8 percent. Authors Frédéric Debruyne and Andreas Dullweber share, "A superior experience helps to earn stronger loyalty among customers, turning them into promoters who tend to buy more, stay longer, and make recommendations to their friends. As a result, promoters have a lifetime value that can reach six to fourteen times that of detractors, depending on the industry."

Suppose we want to see the true impact of how customer obsession impacts a business's bottom line. In that case, there is no better company to turn to than Amazon, whose mission is to be earth's most customer-centric business. Amazon's UK website states," Our mission is to continually raise the bar of the customer experience by using the internet and technology to help consumers find, discover, and buy anything, and empower businesses and content creators to maximize their success."

In a 2007 Harvard Business Review (HBR) article, Julia Kirby and Thomas A. Stewart—two HBR editors—interviewed Jeff Bezos, founder and CEO of Amazon, to learn what's different about the strategy formulation process at Amazon. Bezos detailed the customer obsession culture as a differentiator. He explained that this culture ensures that Amazon is customer-focused rather than being competitor-focused. While Bezos states there is nothing wrong with competitor focus, it is not where Amazon gets its energy. "If you focus on the competitor, you tend to slack off when your benchmarks say that you're the best. But if your focus is on customers, you keep improving." He further explains that being customer-obsessed does not mean that Amazon ignores its competitors; Amazon stays alert to what the competitors are doing and certainly benchmarks things very carefully. But a lot of the energy and drive as both a company and a culture comes from trying to build customer-focused strategies. This strategy and mindset align with the guidelines for the infinite game where Sinek advises us to be mission-focused rather than competitor-focused.

In the interview, Bezos mentions, "Customers want selection, low prices, and fast delivery. This can be different from business to business: There are companies serving other customers who wouldn't put price, for example, in that set. But having found out what those things are for our customers, I can't imagine that ten years from now they are going to say, *'I love Amazon, but if only they could deliver my products a little more slowly.'* And they're not going to, ten years from now, say, *'I really love Amazon, but I wish their prices were a little higher.'* So, we know that when we put energy into defect reduction, which reduces our cost structure and thereby allows lower prices, that will be paying us dividends ten years from now. If we keep putting energy into that flywheel, ten years from now it'll be spinning faster and faster."

Figures published by Statista, a leading provider of market and consumer data, show that Amazon's numbers surpass the 4 percent - 8 percent forecasted by the Bain study. In 2017, Amazon's market share of the US e-commerce retail market was 37 percent, which is further expected to increase significantly by 2021. Amazon's projected market share for 2021 will account for 50 percent of the entire e-commerce retail market's gross merchandise volume (GMV).

The Statista report, published by Tugba Sabanoglu, declared Amazon Prime and Amazon Prime Day as two key features that have significantly contributed to Amazon's ever-rising projection. These are also the same two factors that Bezo's shared in the HBR interview when discussing his customer-obsession strategy. These two features have significantly contributed to Amazon's increased customer spending.

- Amazon Prime, a subscription membership, includes free and faster shipping options as well as exclusive access to proprietary music and video streaming services. The report further states that as of December 2018, 62 percent of Amazon's customers in the United States were Amazon Prime members. This is relevant to Amazon's success as a company, as Prime members are highly engaged shoppers who spend more than double the amount of non-Prime members on the platform per year.

- In 2015, Amazon launched its one-day members-only shopping event Prime Day to celebrate the twentieth anniversary of Amazon's founding. However, this Prime-exclusive event has turned into one of the company's biggest shopping days, rivaling traditional holiday shopping events Black Friday and Cyber Monday in terms of sales. In 2018, Amazon Prime Day sales amounted to $4.19 billion, and on Prime Day, shopper conversion was much higher than the average rate of the preceding quarter.

Statistica data confirms Bezo's hypothesis that selection, low price, and fast delivery do indeed turn Amazon customers into true brand fans.

KEY TAKEAWAYS

In Chapter 4, we discussed empathic arrogance and how it enables us to build better digital products. Throughout this chapter, we took the concept of "customer empathy" to the next level. We start to obsess about our customers' experience across every single touchpoint with our brand. Our obsession is not limited to digital channels such as websites or mobile apps but every single customer touchpoint, as we saw in the Zappos example. And most important of all, customer obsession is not a process but a mindset.

Customer obsession starts with getting the expected customer experience right. This means arriving at a T-Mobile store for an appointment and expecting to be serviced or arriving at an Airbnb and expecting someone to let you in. The basic expected experience earns you a five-star rating. But to grow a true fan base, you have to scale the experience to turn your customer into a brand fan who repeatedly returns to your brand and advocates for it.

Walking through VisualStager's story we observed how customer obsession results in engaged customers who inform you where to focus and what features to build. We also saw how Amazon is leading the e-commerce marketplace with its customer-obsessed culture.

Blind Arrogance	Empathetic Arrogance
What can I do to make this experience better?	What will it take for me to design an experience that makes you literally tell every single person you've ever encountered?
Focusing on the customer at a specific point in time in the customer journey	Obsessing about the customer experience at every point in a customer's interaction with the brand.

Blind Arrogance	Empathetic Arrogance
We know what product features improve business value	We know what product features improve the customer's experience while providing business value
Reading customer persona report to understand the customer	Embedding yourself in the customer community to listen to and observe the customer
Focusing on product performance data to identify new features	Identifying new product features by focusing on the customer to understand problems and using the data to augment understanding

Our customers are at the center of all our products. But what happens when you expand your digital product globally, across other countries? The product has to change, evolve, and adapt to the global market. This is where the concept of the "global consumer" comes in, which we will tackle in the next chapter.

CHAPTER 6

Glocalization, Culturalization & Innovation

———

When you finally think you understand your customer, they start to change—especially as we expand into global markets. The change is not limited to language; it also weaves its way into the small cultural, political, and business nuances. In the United States, my experience with Starbucks, one of my favorite brands, is sometimes a quick coffee, mostly a mobile app order. Yet, at other times, when I hang out with friends or read a book underneath the glowing lights of a Starbucks café, I cannot help but notice the physical places outfitted with a mix of communal tables, lounging chairs as well as small tables that invite customers to hang out and mingle over a cup of coffee. This inviting ambiance carries over to my favorite Starbucks location in Fort, Mumbai, where the Starbucks café has Indian teakwood furniture. The interiors feature works from local craftsmen and artists, and the store's color theme is inspired by the richness of Indian spices.

The menu includes the brand's signature drinks, as well as a blend of local favorites, such as the Alphonso Mango Java Chip Frappuccino® and the Tandoori Paneer (Indian cheese) Sandwich.

In a 2010 article for Reuters, correspondent Lionel Laurent explains how Starbucks changed its café culture in France after years of losses. In 2010, Starbucks had just fifty-four stores in France and annual sales of around 55 million euros ($67.5 million). The operation had lost money yearly since 2004 but turned its first quarterly profit in the last three months of 2009. "We in France don't drink coffee all day long, and flavored coffee is not in our culture," said Bernard Boutboul, head of food retail consultancy Gira Conseil. Because of the French café culture, Starbucks needed to up their game. It introduced the well-known local fare called the café gourmand—a single shot of espresso served with three delicate pastries, including a mango macaroon. Since then, Starbucks has expanded and grown by formulating its menu to fit the needs of the locals without compromising its signature brand. Along with the menu being adapted to meet local tastes, Starbucks' localization strategy also includes innovative store designs, so they are able to fully adapt to the culture of the location.

Glocalization is a combination of the words "globalization" and "localization." In an article on the website Investopedia, Adam Hayes says that the term is used to describe a product or service that is developed and distributed globally but is also adjusted to accommodate the user or consumer in a local market. For example, when I used an Uber in India, I could pay by cash, and when I traveled to Istanbul, Uber provided the additional feature to call a boat. When my sister in India shops for clothes online via Myntra, a popular Indian app, she can pay via credit or cash on delivery, and the items are delivered to her home. But, a small yet imperative operational difference can be easily missed—in India, the same person who delivers one's goods also picks up their returns. This manner of operation is starkly different compared to that found in the US, where we drop off our returns to a USPS, FedEx, or any similar courier service. The differences between the United States and India are clear, especially to me; seeing as I was born and raised there, India is my second home. Yet, these slight differences never fail to surprise me when they are brought to light. When visiting my sister in India, I was surprised when she instructed, "I am leaving some Myntra returns on the kitchen table. Can you please give them to the delivery guy when he stops by?"

When building digital products for a global market, however comfortable you are within the market, it is essential to get even more obsessed with your customer. And this time around, it is not just about the customer; it is also about the surroundings, the culture that seeps into every behavioral element, the political landscape influencing your customer, the competitive barrier and business norms in the new market—and so much more.

HOW CULTURALIZATION IMPACTS DIGITAL PRODUCTS

To understand how global cultures impact digital products, I reached out to Chui Chui Tan, a user experience consultant and "culturalization" expert. Alongside this, Chui Chui is also the founder of Beyo Global—a consulting agency helping companies (such as BBC, Marriott, Google, Spotify, Fiverr, Clarks, and many more) to strategize, build, scale, and operationalize global products.

Chui Chui shared that when your products and services involve global audiences, it adds another layer of complexity to a customer's experience. The differences in cultures, the influences of the political and economic history, the impact of infrastructure setup, and many similar factors shape how a location's society, and, by extension, your local customers will function, behave, want, need, and accept. Culturalization is the process of ensuring that you understand your international markets and customers on various levels that align with your business and industry. You can leverage insights by turning them into concrete, actionable plans that influence your approach to the design, features, marketing, and value proposition of your products and services.

As we dove deeper into how the history of a country impacts user thoughts and actions and, hence, digital products, Chui Chui shared, "Understanding your customers is one thing about the customer themselves. But my approach is much more than just the customers themselves; it also includes the environment and the context they are in. So, whenever I help businesses, we don't look into just what people want and try to walk in their shoes, but also the context around them. For example, I'd question if their politics is influencing how they behave or how they think? This is because there is always a reason behind that triggers certain behaviors or mentalities. It is about having a holistic view of the market, the country, the society, and the individuals."

As we spoke, Chui Chui and I discussed the Philippines *Tingi* culture, as it is partly similar to India. In India, when I grew up, there was no concept of a Costco or buying in bulk; we shopped at neighborhood stores and bought vegetables every day. Chui Chui shared how the Philippines was colonized by Spain for 333 years, became a territory of the US in 1898, and got its independence in 1946. The country has a strong Asian culture enriched by strong western influences — "a highly collectivist, hierarchical & family-oriented society" is how Tan describes it. The "Getting the most out of what I've paid" mentality is strong. "*Ayaw malugi*" a local term that means "don't want to feel cheated." is one unique aspect of the *Tingi* culture that means you can buy cooking oil by the cup, cigarettes by the stick, shampoo by the sachet, garlic in packs of four cloves. This affordable solution results in the locals only buying what they need. But, with the result of what's available, wealthier consumers now simply buy multiple sachets, a habitual & familiar behavior.

To explain how this culture manifests in digital products. Chui Chui shared an example of Spotify, a Swedish audio streaming and media services provider. In the United States, we buy a monthly subscription to its streaming services. However, in India, where customers most often purchase things in small quantities, as they do not want to feel a sense of "I *am buying a lot, but I'm not fully using it.*" Based on the insights and data they gathered from many levels of research, Spotify realized that their standard monthly subscription might not be fit for Indian customers—especially seeing as they carried a mentality of "*I don't think I'll listen to music tomorrow or the day after; therefore, I do not need the service.*" Thus, Spotify made the informed decision to offer Indian customers different plans—they could purchase access to the application on a daily or weekly basis or opt-in for only a limited amount of the paid features available if that's what their budget demanded. Before brainstorming or building solutions, these are the small, minute details you are looking for to understand why people behave the way they do. Therefore, when expanding to global markets, we have to pay attention to not only the users but also the social and political context that influences certain behaviors.

Blind arrogance is when you think your global customer is like your US customer, and what you build for your US customer transcends across the globe.

Blind Arrogance	Empathetic Arrogance
Assumes that a single digital product will work for everyone across the globe.	Understands that a user's actions, as well as the social and political environment, impact digital products

GLOBAL PRODUCTS & RESEARCH IMPACTS

To better understand how research changes as we cross borders, I reached out to Jeanne Liu, a market and user research expert. Jeanne and I met while working for Marriott, where one of Jeanne's responsibilities included global research. When talking about her Marriott experience, Jeanne shared one of her favorite research projects regarding hotel websites. Jeanne traveled with the team to Shanghai, China, and Tokyo, Japan, to better understand how customers perceived the hotel websites. Hotel websites are product-level pages where customers can find detailed hotel information, such as its location and the activities available in the hotel and the areas surrounding it. Additionally, other possibly pertinent details are listed, such as the amenities on offer in the hotel (pools, spas, gyms, etc.) and rooms (coffee machines, mini-fridges, etc.), alongside general check-in/check-out information. Customers can also book a stay from a hotel website.

When you think about booking a stay, there are some common elements: the dates of travel, the city, the hotel address, the total cost of the stay. These elements are always localized with the Marriott and The Ritz-Carlton brand websites and mobile apps, so the date and currency formats align with the country standards. The Marriott team was interested in the imagery, colors, and the missing elements of the hotel detail that make or break it for the customer when they are booking online. Reflecting back, Jeanne recalled how she worked with a local vendor and a great recruiter, who enlisted hotel customers to speak with. Everyone anticipated greatness from this event. Yet, as they started to test, they met one customer who was not on the list of recruited people to speak with. And it was this one person who changed the way they looked at the global websites.

Jeanne recollects her stay at the JW Marriott in Shanghai. Jetlagged, she often worked out in the hotel gym in the early hours of the morning. She noticed a gentleman in the gym working out with her. On late nights, as the team had dinner at the hotel, after a long day of testing, they saw the same gentleman walking around the hotel. On exchanging pleasantries with him, they realized he was the General Manager of the hotel. He lived in the hotel and hence worked long hours. The team introduced themselves as the global product and research teams from the Marriott Headquarters in the US, and they were discussing the localized hotel websites with the local customers. The research plan was focused on talking to current and prospective hotel customers who stayed at Marriott or other local hotels. The research plan did not include talking to the Marriott team that worked at the hotels.

The General Manager shared with the team that he disliked the current hotel website as it did not meet the needs of the local population and forced the hotel to build its own website. Oh no! This was something we, at the headquarters, did not want the local hotels to do. Customers come to the Marriott website and mobile app to book travel. When the hotel is listed on the main Marriott website, it becomes more visible to the customers planning their travels, as these customers do not search for and visit each individual hotel website. Additionally, we implemented new functionalities, such as personalization and in-depth analytics, to see how customers were browsing and interacting with the Marriott website. The local hotel website does not benefit from these features or the marketing investment to drive traffic to the site.

The General Manager explained that in China, Marriott hotel brands are seen as a luxury. Therefore, both customers who stay at the hotel, as well as locals who dine at the hotel, associate dining at the hotel restaurants as an experience. The hotel restaurant is a sought-out venue for special events such as birthdays and weddings. There are dining memberships for the restaurants, and locals like to receive deals and special offers on their special days. The restaurant helps build hotel loyalty (and, eventually, brand loyalty). The current websites for the Marriott hotels did not include detailed web pages for the restaurants, which hindered the hotel staff in meeting customer expectations. This was a big learning for the team as the research approach was focused on the hotel website designs and the booking feature.

After they visited the Marriott in China, the team traveled to Japan. Based on their discoveries from Shanghai, they updated their research approach in Tokyo and intentionally sought out both the hotel staff and the customers. In Japan, the team learned that hotel details are crucial. Customers want to see detailed room layouts, with measurements included. They wanted to know the location of the room and to pick their own. The Tokyo Marriott was competing with local Japanese websites that provide these in-depth booking features.

The research team returned to the corporate headquarters armed with a better understanding of the needs of the Chinese and Japanese markets. In accordance, the product team then prioritized and built features that increased customer satisfaction and enabled hotels to create a true fan following in the local cities and the global market. The current Marriott hotel websites include restaurant-level details. They had learned that when planning for global research, it is important to extend the conversations from what we would consider a traditional user in the US market.

Blind Arrogance	Empathetic Arrogance
When building or scaling a digital product across borders, let's leverage our existing research plan	When building or scaling a digital product that spans borders, we need to rebuild our research plan to include more than current and prospective customers. We need to approach and speak to people who help us understand the local political, social, and business landscapes

PLANNING FOR STRATEGIC GLOBAL GROWTH

We are aware of China's internet censored market. Many leading American digital firms, including Google, Amazon, eBay, and Uber, have successfully expanded internationally by introducing their products, services, and platforms in other countries. However, they have failed in China, the world's largest digital market. In a comprehensive five-year study, Feng Li published her research paper in 2018 in the Academy of Management Discoveries, where she systematically identifies the reasons behind the failures of major Western digital firms in China. She also published an overview in the *Harvard Business Review* (HBR).

In her study, Li used two rounds of interviewing to identify the "inside view" and the "outside view" of the phenomenon.

The first round of interviews focused on the "inside view". The inside view is analyzing the problem based on what you know about the current process and the information you have at hand. To determine the inside view Li met with forty senior business executives from companies that are close to digital products and expansion. Included in the study were six leading Western digital firms (Google, Yahoo, eBay, Amazon, Groupon, and Uber) and their corresponding direct competitors in China (Baidu, Sohu, Taobao, JD.com, Meituan, and Didi). The insights gleaned that the main cause of failure was lack of strategic knowledge and patience by the Western digital firms.

The second round of interviews were planned around the "outside view" where Li drew comparisons from the outside and brought in information from how others have fared when attempting to solve similar problems. Interviews with 185 seasoned expert observers in China highlighted the failure by Western digital firms to conform to China's business environment as the main cause of their failure. Li says, "It led to a series of competitive disadvantages, thereby allowing Chinese digital firms to race ahead in the fight for market share."

Drawing insights from the combined findings of both the inside and outside view interviews, the key learnings that emerged were:

1. Poor understanding of the business environment

2. Ineffective strategy making and communication, and

3. Underperformance in operation and execution.

On filtering the research insights by the *digital product point of view*, the insights that stand out are:

- Lack of a deep understanding of the Chinese market

- Ill-fated attempts to impose global business models unsuited to the Chinese market

- Failure to cope with the extremely fierce competition in China with a large number of determined local competitors

- Imposing technological platforms developed for the US market on China

- Underestimating the major differences between digital business and other industries

- Ineffective innovation strategies

In her research, Li summarized that while Western multinationals from other sectors benefit from advanced technologies, established product lines, and global supply chains that may take Chinese firms years of investment to catch up to, digital firms do not. They operate in an environment where the barriers to entry are relatively low. The competitive focus should be on product and business model innovations and service delivery rather than the most advanced technologies.

Feng Li's research, examples shared by Chui Chui, Jeanne and my personal experiences with cultures, countries, and the digital landscape, lead me to believe that to break into a new global market, we will have to ingrain ourselves in the local culture so we can better learn and observe from our customers. We will have to understand international markets more thoroughly and explore new business models. We cannot blindly assume that two human beings in two corners of the planet share the same exact needs and work in the same exact surroundings. To study digital products that have successfully scaled across the globe, I searched for an example to help understand the global nuances; the app that most stood out was TikTok.

On the App Store, TikTok describes their offering as, "*A personalized video feed based on what you watch, like, and share. TikTok offers you real, interesting, and fun videos that will make your day. You'll find a variety of videos from Food and Fashion to Sports and DIY—and everything in between.*" In August 2020, TikTok revealed specific US and global growth milestones for the first time in a lawsuit against the United

States government, challenging them over an effective ban on the application that they had set to be implemented in September 2020. On the CNBC website, Alex Sherman reported that as of August 2020, TikTok had about 100 million monthly active US users, up nearly eight hundred percent from January 2018. TikTok also revealed that the app has been downloaded around two billion times globally and is visited by about fifty million daily active users in the United States alone. How did an app from China grow at this speed globally?

In a September 2019 article for Harvard Business Review (HBR) titled "The Strategy Behind TikTok's Global Rise," Rebecca Fannin, a journalist covering China's entrepreneurial boom, delves deeper into TikTok's exponential success. In the article Fannin shares that in just two years since its launch, TikTok has emerged to rival companies like Netflix, YouTube, Snapchat, and Facebook with more than one billion downloads in 150 markets worldwide and seventy-five languages. From the 2020 statistics above, we can clearly notice that the app continued to grow at a rapid pace. In the article, Fannin shares that Zhang Yiming, the CEO of ByteDance, the company that owns TikTok is also a former Microsoft engineer and a Chinese serial entrepreneur who had the vision from the start of running a company that would expand beyond borders and would span the globe.

One key element of the app that has helped it scale is that TikTok requires minimal translation. Often when we scale a product to other countries, language is the first barrier; given my experience of working with global products while at Marriott, I can attest that the operational and translation costs are often what slows down the scaling process for a product. TikTok's foresight when building the app has helped surpass its growth as compared to other Chinese apps such as the messaging service WeChat. Outside of China, WeChat is used predominantly within Chinese communities to keep in touch with friends and families in China and, therefore, has a minimal need to be translated for global markets. TikTok's universal design and broad accessibility drastically cut down on the translation-related process and costs, thus enabling the app to grow exponentially.

A second key component that has potentially harbored Tik-Tok's growth is that, despite Zhang's efforts to present Dou-yin and TikTok as the same product, they may likely be two separate apps in actuality. In a 2019 article on the website ChinaSocialMedia.net, the author "Rocco" points out that TikTok is the international version of the booming Chinese short video app, Douyin. "Rocco" further states that depending on the app store you use, you will either be able to download Douyin or TikTok—users in China can only see Douyin listed, whereas users of the overseas App Store or Google Play Store will only find TikTok available for download.

The fact that the apps are, in reality, two separate entities becomes clear when running the same search term in both of them. For example, one of TikTok's most popular influencers—at the time of writing—goes by the handle "Lisaand-dLena," a verified account by two German twins with over thirty-two million followers. However, when you enter "LisaandLena" into Douyin's search bar, the only result is an unverified account with 102 followers, containing seven videos. When swapping apps and inversing the test, the results are strikingly similar. One of Douyin's most popular accounts is that of Chinese actor Chen He, who has over fifty-two million follows and features sixty-two videos. However, when searching the same name on TikTok, several unverified accounts come up instead, all of which contain similar videos to those found on Chen He's Douyin account. He further shares that the overseas iPhone version also does not have the same Apple Wallet functions the Chinese version has.

Zhang's strategy of dual apps, one for China's internet censored market and another app for the rest of the world, could be a new business model for other digital content companies aiming for such global reach—including China-based digital start-ups with new ambitions to venture out beyond the home market.

Now that we understand how local markets differ and why it is equally important to understand our "global user," I want to turn to the concept of "timing." Seeing as the global marketplace is shrinking, what is the right time to think on a global level? When should you plan to incorporate and implement global products in your business? Based on the case study of TikTok, I would say that the right time to act is at the moment of conception—when you first define the product value proposition. Because if you want to scale your product, you have to be sure the brand messaging and its application can span across borders. Plus, it also changes the way you architect the solution. My conversation with Chui Chui also bolstered my understanding. Chui Chui suggests it's about changing people's and companies' mindsets. "We need them to understand they can't keep saying they aren't ready to go global. When you build a product to only compete with one market, you'll eventually need to entirely rebuild that product to fit the global market."

Blind Arrogance	Empathetic Arrogance
We will think about expanding the product when we are ready	Let's discuss the vision and plan for this product. If we want to expand it globally, we will have to strategize our approach and build it at its very foundation

KEY TAKEAWAYS

If you think digital wars are limited to the United States, you are wrong. As companies expand across global markets, the digital wars are only getting more and more complex. TikTok's story of its global expansion reinforces the fact that the best time to discuss global expansion is the instant we first start to determine and construct the product value proposition.

Chui Chui and Feng Li's study scratches the surface of global nuances. Taking a digital product global is no longer a play on localization but rather involves understanding and navigating the social, political, and business landscapes. And last but not least, the players for global products are different from those found in the United States, as could be seen in Jeanne's story.

The concepts of "empathetic arrogance" and "customer obsession" discussed in chapters five and six also apply to a global perspective. As you scale your product to unknown territories, it is more important than ever that you take an empathetic arrogant approach. Be aware of your blind spots. Be empathetic when understanding the global customer—who differs heavily from your domestic one. When designing the experience, walk through the experience ideation exercise (the one we learned from Brian Chesky in the introduction) **twice**—once for your domestic audience and again for your domestic users. Understand when the experiences converge and when they diverge—this can inform you how to build and scale your product.

Blind Arrogance	Empathetic Arrogance
Every human is like all other humans	Every human is like some and maybe no other human
Assuming that a single digital product will work for everyone across the globe	Understanding not just the user's actions but also the social and political environment that surrounds them
We will think about expanding the product when we are ready	Let's discuss the vision and plan for this product. If we want to expand it globally, we will have to strategize an approach and build it at its very foundation

Blind Arrogance	Empathetic Arrogance
When building or scaling a digital product across borders, let's leverage our existing research plan	When building or scaling a digital product that spans borders, we need to rebuild our research plan to include more than current and prospective customers. We need to approach and talk to people who can help us understand the local political, social, and business landscapes

When defining your product value proposition, discuss future plans for the product. If you see the product expanding to other countries, make plans to talk to global customers and stakeholders. Obsess about your global customer. When building the product, take globalization into account at every step of the developmental product lifecycle—at conception, when discussing features, and when creating the product.

PART III

EMPATHETIC ARROGANCE

BUILDING THE DIGITAL PRODUCT FOR THE CUSTOMER
In Parts I and II, we focused on the need for empathy and compassion when building digital products. But being empathetic is not sufficient. In this age of digital Darwinism, digital product builders have to deal with audacious problems that may sometimes lead us to doubt our capabilities and yet, at other times, have complete confidence in our methods. To build what is suitable for our customers, we need empathetic arrogance.

In chapter one, "Digital Darwinism," we saw how digital products evolved from technology to include user experience. Then as digital disrupted existing business models, business foresight and marketing insight crept into the world of digital products. And as digital products started to understand user behavior, both on their proprietary platforms as well as third-party digital platforms, data became king. With more data, we were able to model data to understand the user and provide personalized experiences.

In this section of the book, we delve deeper into each of these four components of digital products— marketing, design, technology, and data. While each one of the four components is equally important, deep, and dense, and books have been written to address each component individually, my focus is for you, as the product builder, to walk away from a basic understanding of how the four components come together to build a digital product.

As we discuss each component, you will notice the components do not live in isolation but instead intertwine. A good product sits at the intersection of the four components. Each chapter in this part will examine common pitfalls of product teams and how we can use empathetic arrogance over blind arrogance to build the best product for our customers.

CHAPTER 7

Single View of the Customer

————

A few years back, I ordered organic hair color from a website based in the UK. I think it must have popped up in my Google search results at some point, as it was not a website I had visited before. The product arrived, I used it, and I forgot about the order. A few weeks later, I received some emails whose content was geared toward cancer patients and survivors. I then checked the address that the emails were being sent from, speculating it was spam. Upon visiting the website, I realized the emails came from the same website where I had ordered the organic hair color. On my second visit to the website, I noticed the company's mission was to be the destination for people living with long-term conditions who require everyday practical support for their symptoms and side effects. There was a disconnect between the product and marketing teams, as, on the webpage listing details for the hair color, there was no reference to cancer or related health conditions. But clearly, the marketing team assumed that everyone who bought the hair color was a cancer patient or survivor. I did not visit the website again.

Business is like a two-sided coin. You need a great product, and then you need effective marketing to help customers understand the product value proposition. However, the customer experience across both the digital product and all marketing channels has to be consistent, in contrast to the example I shared above. Our product and marketing teams have to have the same view of the customer. If your digital product is not aligned with how you market it, you have lost the customer.

When we think about the experience across a company, a customer does not break up their separate experience by channel. They expect a seamless experience when they interact with a brand at any touch point. To deliver this, companies need a single view of the customer across all customer-facing teams—this includes, but is not limited to, every digital product, marketing tactic, brick-and-mortar location (such as the T-Mobile experience I mentioned in Chapter 5), and company call center. A single view of the customer enables companies to understand and better engage with customers by knowing who they are and what they are looking for. It acts as the single source of information about your customers. It gives you the ability to analyze past behavior in order to better target and personalize future customer interactions. This is especially true across product and digital marketing as they are both digital customer-facing channels, and the customer journey from marketing to the final product must be seamless.

Using increasingly granular data, from customer click-streams, detailed demographics, and psychographics, companies are creating highly customized offers that steer customers to the "right" merchandise or services—at the right moment, at the right price, and in the right channel. But trying to develop a single view of the customer is easier said than done, especially for companies where product and marketing teams do not co-exist. According to a White Paper published by Experian in 2015, based on a survey of 1,000 global marketers conducted by the team, 89 percent said they had experienced difficulties *creating* a *Single Customer View*.

This difficulty is a more common problem across teams than you would think. When researching this book, I spoke to my friend Dave, who leads a product team at a Fortune 500 company. He shared that one of his biggest pain points was that his view of the customer was very different from his colleague, who ran a parallel product line. The customer started on Dave's product, and once he narrowed down an item to purchase, he was directed to the check-out cart that his colleague managed. He shared, "We never actually had a unified perspective of the customer. Instead, it kind of happens by the default lowest common denominator." This example of Dave and his colleague displays communication between two products teams, which should be easier when compared with the process of obtaining a uniform view of the customer across different teams in different departments (such as product and marketing, for example).

Today's digital customer is informed, they have the internet at their fingertips to search and purchase what they are looking for. To build a strong relationship with our customers across these digital channels, how can we make sure that the customer has a consistent, flawless experience with the brand across every digital touchpoint—the digital product and the marketing channels.

A UNIFIED PERSPECTIVE

One of my product teams was tasked with refreshing content and functionality on an existing website to meet the needs of a marketing campaign. With multiple internal stakeholders and tight timelines, the team went about making updates in an effective and efficient manner. They walked through the customer journey to ensure the changes felt right and resonated with the customers.

At the end of the quarter, with the mindset to improve the experience for future campaigns, the product team met with the marketing team to understand the impact of the product changes on the campaign performance. They were especially interested to learn the following: How did customers find the web page(s)? Did they see a Google Ad? Did they find the link from the home page or an email? Did they come across it organically via Google search results? Once they had access to the website, how many customers viewed the physical product(s) listed on the page? How does that figure compare to the number of customers who proceeded to buy the product? The performance numbers for both teams did not align; after suffering much frustration from trying to understand what they were missing, they reached out for help. I had a few questions for both teams. First and foremost, did they have a common understanding of the customer and how to appeal to them? Secondly, did the teams align on how they would determine if the campaign was successful? No. Both teams worked independently based on their understanding of who the customer was and how they measured success.

If we keep building the product with a heads-down approach while the marketing team continues to market the product, we will lose the customer. It is the same customer who is engaging with us on our product—our website or app or in-home device—or engaging with content on social media channels, emails, or notifications.

Andy Acs and Konrad Waliszewski, the founders of a travel app, TripScout, learned the same lesson in the early days of their start-up. TripScout is a travel app geared toward travelers who dream about creating their own customized itinerary when traveling. The app enables travelers to save points of interest from 100 million local destinations and stitch together a perfect, fully personalized travel itinerary.

Andy and Konrad first met at American University in Washington DC, where Andy was studying for his undergraduate degree in Business Administration. After graduating, the cofounders kept in touch, frequently meeting over dinner to talk about travel. Both Konrad and Andy continued to travel, though Andy did not travel as often as Konrad, who had traveled to nearly one hundred countries. During their conversations, Andy and Konrad discussed their observation of the changing trends in travel. On their individual travels, they both noticed that, like them, most millennials did not want to explore via package tours, get on a bus, or walk around with a group of strangers. Travel was transforming into an activity fueled by gaining an appreciation for a new place instead of visiting a preordained list of sights or landmarks.

Andy and Konrad spent time talking to travelers to observe and learn how they planned their visits. They asked travelers if they could watch them as they planned their trip or if the travelers could please take a video as they explored travel and talk through the trip planning and inspiration process. The duo continued to brainstorm and discuss how they bring this new traveling experience to digital, as a website or app.

When Konrad traveled, he found the best tour guides, went on their walking tours, and asked if the guides could record the tour in short two or four-minute bits. The first TripScout app that launched in 2015 was basically city walking tours for top traveled cities, with Konrad, a DC native, narrating the Washington DC tour. When observing the travelers' plans, Andy and Konrad noticed that the very first thing people did after saying something like, "Oh, I want to go take a trip to Iceland," was not typing "Iceland" into Google—they were typing it into Instagram. Thus, they realized that travel search was shifting from one platform to another.

This learning spurred two insights for the cofounders. The first—they could build the best travel app, but if they did not know where their customers are, in this case searching on Instagram for inspiration and not Google search as they had assumed, they would lose these would-be travelers. Secondly, the duo realized that they had to figure out the marketing before they built and grew the product. They needed to know how to meet their customers where they were, which in this case was across social media platforms.

The onset of the COVID-19 pandemic strained many industries, but perhaps no area of the US economy was hit harder than the travel industry—this also just so happened to be the best time for Andy and Konrad to connect even more securely to their audience of would-be travelers. They strategized their marketing efforts to grow their audience. Along with heading up the TripScout website, they laid the foundation for their social media presence over Instagram, TikTok, and Facebook. They pulled articles and videos from top global publishers and content from local Instagram influencers to provide travel details on more than 100 destinations worldwide. Users can save any restaurant, tourist attraction, or other points of interest with one tap, allowing trip planners to easily create a personalized itinerary. They began producing a "Travel from Home" video series where the company interviewed various travel celebrities, Michelin-starred chefs, vloggers, and more, having two to three live virtual events a week.

In a March 2021 interview with Jim Dallke, the associate editor at Chicago InnoThough, Waliszewski shared that though travel in 2020 had been on the decline with the COVID-19 pandemic, TripScout's social strategy paid off; their Instagram following had grown from one million the previous year to over three million followers. "Attention and engagement are the most valuable and hardest-to-get currency in travel. Even though people are not traveling, they're still thinking about travel, probably even more than before."

Andy, a product manager by training, led product teams at Living Social and WeddingWire. As I spoke to Andy, he shared, "Companies build better products when marketing and product are tightly coupled. Because you need to have the same view of who the customer is. One of the things that we have shifted in our mindset is that Instagram is no longer a marketing channel. Instagram is a product of ours. Those are our customers. They're just interacting with us on a different interface."

I share a similar mindset with my product teams. As digital product builders, we cannot be focused on just the bottom half of the marketing funnel. Obsessing with the customers means understanding customer behavior at every part of their journey, including the acquisitions or top half of the marketing funnel.

A collective but single view of the customer across teams ensures you have the customer.

Blind Arrogance	Empathetic Arrogance
The product team understands the customer	All teams - whether they work on marketing, product, experience, or technology, have the same view and understanding of the customer

WORKING BACKWARD

Two approaches stand out when aligning teams across product and marketing. The first one is the *"Working Backward"* approach; Ian McAllister, Director of Amazon Day and former Director of Amazon Smile, shared this approach on Quora a few years ago. In the May 2012 post on a Quora article, he shares that at Amazon, the product teams try to work backward from the customer instead of starting with the idea of a product and then trying to tack customers to it. While, in his article, Ian shares that this approach works well for new products and features, I suggest also trying this backward approach for an existing product or feature to ensure that the teams are aligned on how they are approaching the problem and talking about it.

In the article, Ian shares, "For a new initiative, a product manager typically starts by writing an internal press release announcing the finished product. The target audience for the press release is the new/updated product's customers, which can be retail customers or internal users of a tool or technology. Internal press releases are centered around the customer problem, how current solutions (internal or external) fail, and how the new product will blow away existing solutions. If the benefits listed don't sound very interesting or exciting to customers, then perhaps they're not (and shouldn't be built). Instead, the product manager should keep iterating on the press release until they've come up with benefits that actually sound like benefits. Iterating on a press release is a lot less expensive than iterating on the product itself (and quicker!)."

When using this "working backward" approach with existing products, you may learn one of three things - first, you are killing it with the product. Your customers get the product, and all is well. Or secondly, you might realize that you are not telling the right story and, therefore, need to modify the messaging. And, most challenging of all, you may realize that your ascertained solution is not solving the customer's problem— and thus, you will need to pivot to find another solution.

Here's an example outline for the press release. A key thing to keep in mind when drafting the press release is that though the press release is an internal document, its target audience is your customer.

- **Heading** - Name the product in a way the reader (i.e., your target demographic) will understand.

- **Sub-Heading** - Describe who the market for the product is and what benefit they get. One sentence only, placed underneath the title.

- **Summary** - Give a summary of the product and the benefit. Assume it is the only thing the reader will engage with.

- **Problem** - Describe the problem your product solves.

- **Solution** - Describe how your product elegantly solves the problem.

- **Quote from You** - A quote from a spokesperson in your company.

- **How to Get Started** - Describe how easy it is to get started.

- **Customer Quote** - Provide a quote from a hypothetical customer that describes how they experienced the benefit.

- **Closing and Call to Action** - Wrap it up and give pointers where the reader should go next.

This internal press release must be a page and a half at most. If the press release is more than a page and a half, it is probably too long. Keep it simple—three to four sentences for most paragraphs. Ian suggests an accompanying Frequently Asked Questions (FAQ) section to the press release if there are questions that need to be addressed for stakeholders.

As Ian shares in his article, "Once the project moves into development, the press release can be used as a touchstone, a guiding light. The product team can ask themselves, 'Are we building what is in the press release?' If they find they're spending time building things that aren't in the press release (overbuilding), they need to ask themselves why. This keeps product development focused on achieving the customer benefits and not building extraneous stuff that takes longer to build, takes resources to maintain, and doesn't provide real customer benefit (at least not enough to warrant inclusion in the press release)."

Starting the process backward with marketing first to understand what you are building and only then transitioning to how it will be communicated helps build deeper collaboration between cross-functional teams, even before the product building has kicked off. It also ensures that you are indeed making the right product. If the *Product Doomsday* team had followed this "working backward" approach, they would have noticed the messaging gaps sooner in the process and maybe realized they did not have a complete understanding of the customer and the problem.

WORKING FRONTWARD

Now that you have an idea about what you are building and why, I suggest using the "Lean Canvas" approach to align on problems, solutions, key metrics, and competitive advantages. This approach yet again helps to align product and marketing teams. But most importantly, it enables you to identify how you will measure and track success across teams as well as lay the foundation for your marketing plans.

Unlike a business plan—which takes too long to write, and more importantly, no one reads—a Lean Canvas is designed to help you create a quick snapshot of your idea, share it with someone for feedback, and refine it iteratively. On his website, Leanstack.com, assessed in March 2021, Ash Maurya shares that he created the Lean Canvas in 2012 by adapting the original Business Model Canvas by Alexander Osterwalder. The Lean Canvas gives you an actionable and entrepreneur-focused business plan. **What is unique about the Lean Canvas is that the left half of the canvas deals with the product itself, while the right half of the canvas focuses on marketing the product.** This makes it easy for product and marketing teams to collaborate and understand how they will work together.

Here is an outline of the lean canvas:

- **Problem** - Describe the problem your product solves. Use the problem as defined in the press release above.

- **Solution** - Describe how your product elegantly solves the problem. Use the solution as defined in the press release above.

- **Key Metrics** - Describe how you will measure success. When building the product or feature, it's essential to make sure you are capturing these metrics.

In chapter ten, "The Complete Data Story," we will discuss vanity metrics and clarity metrics. After you have read the chapter, I suggest you come back to this exercise and the product work collectively on this to ensure we are identifying the right clarity metrics, the team makes sure they write the tracking code and identifies stakeholders who will be tracking the performance, and how the metrics are pulled to understand the entire customer journey, and not just a snapshot of a moment in time.

- **Unique Value Proposition**: What differentiates your solution from other competitors? Your Unique Value

Proposition should communicate why you are different and worth getting attention. It should be short and ideally fit into a Twitter headline (160 characters or less). This also helps the marketing teams in compiling the right product messaging that sells the product.

- **Unfair Advantage**: Maurya describes **unfair advantage** as something that's developed over time and can't be easily gained. He acknowledges that a start-up's first few Lean Canvas plans will likely not have anything to add to this box, but over time the company's unfair advantage will become clear.

- **Channels**: How will you engage with your customers. In the example of TripScout, this exercise would spell out the social media channels and website.

- **Customer Segments:** List target customers and/or users. Using the SNHU example from Chapter 3, pull in knowledge about your ideal customers here. In today's digital marketing age, this is key to ensuring that both the product and marketing teams use the same consistent messaging to identify and appeal to different customer segments. An example of this process being mishandled is the previously discussed mishap I experienced with the organic hair color company.

- **Cost Structure:** List all costs associated with the business, including fixed and variable fees.

- **Revenue Streams:** List and monitor all avenues of revenue.

I suggest using this approach before you start work on new features. But it is not too late to use the Lean Canvas on existing products. It will help align cross-functional teams on the customer, the problem, how you plan to reach out to the customers, and how you will track and measure success. While the "working backward" method helps the team determine the product's value proposition and conceptualize critical features, the Lean Canvas helps both product and marketing teams determine key metrics, marketing strategies, and revenue streams. Therefore, I suggest teams start with the "working backward" method and then flesh out the marketing details with the Lean Canvas.

KEY TAKEAWAYS

In chapter one, "Digital Darwinism," we saw how a digital product is comprised of four components: understanding of the business, which includes marketing, the customer experience, technology, and data. In chapter five, "Obsessed. Maniacal. Radical. WoW," we discussed how customer experience with the brand is vital and that it has to be consistent across every customer touchpoint. Let's put these two points together: if you want to build a consistent experience for the customer, you have to be intentional. Consistent and flawless customer experience cannot be an afterthought.

Empathetic arrogance is ensuring that all teams—whether it is marketing, experience, technology, or data, have the same view and understanding of the customer. The best time to ensure alignment is before you build a new product; the next best time is *now*.

Blind Arrogance	Empathetic Arrogance
The product team understands the customer	All teams—whether it is marketing, product, experience, or technology, have the same view and understanding of the customer.
We will figure out the product marketing after we build the product.	Both product and marketing teams work collaboratively to understand the customer, the market, and the product. This ensures a holistic view of the product, the customer, and the complete customer journey.

CHAPTER 8

Design with Intent

In 1996, when asked if there was a well-designed product that inspired him, Steve Jobs picked a washing machine. He got more thrill out of evaluating and critiquing washing machines than he had out of any piece of high tech in years. His family did not have a very good washer-dryer, and for about two weeks, the family discussed the old washer-dryer every night at the dinner table. While the talk was about design, it also took into account their values as a family. While American washers are faster, they use more water and detergent as compared to European washers. "Did we care most about getting our wash done in an hour versus an hour and a half? Or did we care most about our clothes feeling really soft and lasting longer? Did we care about using a quarter of the water?"

In the end, the European brand Miele won as the family leaned toward lesser water and detergent. This discussion shows that design is not limited to fancy new gadgets. Every object used by a human can count toward a great design conversation.

"Design is a funny word. Some people think design means how it looks. But of course, if you dig deeper, it's really how it works. The design of the Mac wasn't what it *looks* like, although that was part of it. Primarily, it was how it worked. To design something really well, you have to get it. You have to really grok what it's all about. It takes a passionate commitment to understand really thoroughly something, chew it up, not just quickly swallow it. Most people don't take the time to do that."

This story is from a 1996 interview with Gary Wolf, in which Jobs reflects on why more products are not made with the aesthetics of great design. To Jobs, creativity is about connecting things, grokking, and thoroughly, passionately, and empathetically understanding what you are designing.

The broader one's understanding of the human experience, the better design we will have.

WHEN DESIGN IS THE PROBLEM

I experienced the power of design when working with a product team responsible for a customer-facing digital merchandizing platform. Merchants listed their physical products on this platform, where customers browse and purchase. Think of it like an Amazon or a Groupon, but on a smaller scale. As we dived into the product performance data, we noticed some anomalies. The customer browsing data showed a highly engaged customer base, which meant customers were browsing or looking for products. But the conversion rate was meager. While customers were browsing products, not many customers were purchasing products. We heard from some suppliers that their sales were low or almost null.

The team assumed that the underperforming products were not in demand. We suggested to the suppliers, "Your products are not in demand, try offering a sale price or a different variation of the product." But this was indeed not the problem. Despite our attempt to lower prices, we were unable to move the needle for these suppliers. After digging deeper into the data, guess what we discovered? The problem was the design.

A customer purchase journey spans multiple steps. For this example, let us assume that the hypothesized e-commerce site sells books. In order for the customer to buy a book, they will commonly:

- Browse the variety of products within that specific category; for example, if the customer is searching by genre and interested in books on vegan recipes, they may browse books within the cooking genre

- Check out product details; for example, once the customer identifies a potential book on Thai cuisine, they might be interested in an excerpt that tells them more about the book, the cost of the book, reviews, etc.

- Compare products and check reviews

- Save a product for later review

- Purchase a product, if they like what they see

The goal is to ensure the customer is aware of the variety or categories of products you sell, show them options in a specific category, show them the product's details, and let them purchase. For example, if I am shopping for a book, I may shop in two ways:

- Either I know the exact book I want to buy, I search for it, find it, and buy it.

- Or, I may browse the "shop" until I find a book that meets my needs and then purchase it.

A practice pretty common across organizations is to split the customer journey across multiple product teams. For example, while Team A is responsible for the "browse" feature where customers browse for the products to gain awareness of what is available, Team B focuses on the "search" feature where, instead of browsing, the customer searches for the product—much like the ubiquitous Google or Amazon search boxes. Meanwhile, Team C is responsible for the physical product details, and Team D oversees the final phase of the process, wherein the customer purchases your product.

In the example I shared above, the product team responsible for the browse functionality repeatedly touted their numbers, indicating that customers were engaged. They were browsing and searching for products. Team A was exceeding its projected results. But, as we put the data for the entire customer journey together, the data shared by the team responsible for the purchase experience, Team D, had a comparatively dismal conversion rate. For example, if 1000 users were browsing for the product, only one or two users would end up actually buying it.

To understand where we were losing the customer, the team worked to identify the objectives of this customer journey; we narrowed it down to three essential metrics:

- **Product Category Views**: Are the customers able to find various categories? Building on the bookstore example, are customers browsing children's books, mystery thrillers, technical books, periodicals? While it is true that not all categories will receive an equal amount of engagement, will customers be able to find what they are looking for within the majority of common genres or areas of interest?

- **Customer Purchase Behavior with Focus on Discounted Items**: For customers searching within a specific category, are they able to see and understand the discounted offer? For example, if there is a special 25 percent discount on a book offered by supplier A, compared to supplier B, that are selling the same thing at a standard price—are customers able to see the difference and pick the lower-priced book?

- **Browsing to Purchase Behavior:** For customers who are browsing specific product categories, are they purchasing a product? For example, if I am browsing children's books, am I buying one?

Once we dug into the detailed customer browsing data, we learned that:

- Approximately 70 percent of customers who arrived on the page browsed the categories. The categories higher on the page got more views than those listed lower on the page. Only 5 percent of these customers scrolled the length of the page and browsed the categories listed at the bottom of the page, which indicated that the customer was unable to find the categories that were not prominently displayed on the page.

- When searching for products within a category, customers were repeatedly purchasing the higher priced items even when the same product was listed at a lower price, clearly showing that they could not differentiate between the products.

- For the browsed categories, though customers had viewed certain products, they did not proceed to purchase them— which led us to question if we had the most effective product details on the page.

The design had failed the customer as they could not execute either of the key tasks that the site for designed for.

The data helped us identify some quick wins. For example, all categories must have equal weight in design so customers can see what we sell, and we must improve the sale experience so customers can see what is on sale. While the data told us what was not working, we went back to talk to the customers to understand and observe their shopping behavior to understand how they shop, see how the digital landscape plays a role in the shopping experience, and ascertain why these specific features mentioned above were not working for them.

The lesson I learned was that we have to design with intent. Design is more than a pretty element; it spurs customer action. Set clear objectives for your design before you get started. Identify what you expect the customer to accomplish and then track performance to ensure customers are indeed able to complete the tasks. Secondly, look at the customer journey holistically and do not focus on just one customer action in time.

Blind Arrogance	Empathetic Arrogance
Design is the "pretty" element in a digital product	Design is the functional element in a digital product that spurs action
The product usage data meets our team objectives	The customer behavioral data helps us understand and improve the product experience

DIGITAL DESIGN IS NOT A GARNISH BUT A KEY INGREDIENT

A digital design done right has the power to impact user behavior. In a February 2020 article titled "How Digital Design Impacts User Behavior" in the Harvard Business Review, Shlomo Benartzi—Professor of Behavioral Decision Making at UCLA Anderson School of Management—and Saurabh Bhargava—Associate Professor of Economics at Carnegie Mellon University—provide multiple cases that reveal how many organizations undervalue the power of digital design; they treat it as a garnish versus a key ingredient.

Design on any type of website is a vital element for helping people reach the desired product; this is especially true for products in healthcare. Having an effective healthcare plan that we can afford, and that will provide us with comprehensive coverage, gives us some much-needed peace of mind. However, purchasing healthcare online can be a very daunting task. In the last several years, US consumers have been inundated with the choice of multiple health plans. Whether through public exchanges associated with Medicare Part D or the Affordable Care Act (ACA) or through employer-sponsored exchanges, people are increasingly choosing health plans from a daunting menu of online options.

In the study with George Loewenstein at Carnegie Mellon University, Shlomo and Saurabh sought to understand how labels or wording on a website affected the financial efficiency of people's decisions. They ran a series of online tests in which they asked online subjects to select a health plan from a menu of three alternatives whose prices and cost-sharing features were informed by actual plans available through the Affordable Healthcare Act (ACA).

Given the complexity of ACA, a notable feature of the ACA was to organize health plans into distinct "metal" tiers (think bronze, silver, gold, platinum) defined by the generosity of their actuarial coverage. These "metal" plans range from bronze plans (higher out-of-pocket expense, lower premium) to platinum plans (lower out-of-pocket expense, higher premium).

In their study, Shlomo and Saurabh tested the current "metal" plans against two alternate label options:

- Current: Metal tiers presently used by the ACA (e.g., bronze, silver, platinum)

- Alternate option 1: Generic descriptors (plan A, plan B, plan C)

- Alternate option 2: Words that emphasize the expected medical use most appropriate for each plan (high use, medium use, low use).

The tests showed the following results:

- Many people tend to make poor and costly decisions across all three labeling strategies. They select plans that aren't aligned with their everyday health needs and tolerance for financial risk. Their research suggests that the current design of the ACA, however well-intentioned, may have led to the most inefficient plan choices.

On average, their experimental subjects overspent by an amount equivalent to 24 percent of the typical premium.

- For the "metal" plans, users associated the metal with the quality of care they receive. For example, platinum implies the best plan. They speculate that when faced with the tiered labels (bronze, silver, etc.), consumers selected plans not based on how they expect to use the plan but instead draw inferences about the quality of care they would receive.

- The labels emphasizing or communicating a consumer's expected medical use—high use, medium use, low use - led to significantly better choices than the "metal" labels. While many consumers still chose sub-optimal plans, the medical use labels reduced average excess spending by 37 percent relative to the metal labels.

The key point here is that the design of digital products is a crucial factor, and even a small example of how we categorize and use labels can impact how customers make their decisions. In the case of health insurance plans, labels should serve as signifiers of expected utilization rather than quality.

Empathetic arrogance is fully, passionately, and empathetically under-standing the situation,

then designing, testing, and repeating until you get it right.

Blind Arrogance	Empathetic Arrogance
It is just the design. We have a great technical solution	The broader one's understanding of the human experience, the better design we will have

Companies need stronger design capabilities than ever before, as the best design performers increase their revenue and shareholder returns at nearly twice the rate of their industry counterparts (Sheppard et al. 2019). But, achieving good design is a substantially difficult feat, despite the obvious commercial benefits of designing great products and services. Only the very best designs now stand out from the crowd, given the rapid rise in consumer expectations driven by the likes of Amazon, instant access to global information and reviews, and the blurring of lines between hardware, software, and services.

DESIGN WITH YOUR CUSTOMERS

On an episode of the podcast *Humanizing Data*, Naomi Starr—Managing Director of Dublin-based research firm Core—argues that we often approach research to validate a hypothesis. We assume a solution exists, and we use the research to have our customers provide feedback on this solution. This presumption introduces bias and prevents us from exploring alternate solutions to the problem. She suggests we try new approaches; where, in addition to quantitative techniques (reading data to understand gaps) or the use of focus groups (asking users to provide feedback to a design), we ask users to participate in problem-solving exercises. In the podcast, Naomi says, "Any opportunity to encourage humans to respond emotionally will be more powerful than analyzing a data point based on an assumed logical action. Within these moments, it is possible to realize the nuances of a topic, facilitate conversations about sensitive topics and see the emotion in a person's eyes. "

I had an opportunity to talk with Stephanie Slobodian, who has experience in leading teams and designing user experiences for companies and organizations such as Amazon, Google, Marriott, IBM, National Public Radio (NPR), Gucci, Hallmark, Mercedes Benz, and USAA. I met up with Stephanie to discuss the "co-creation" method—where customers participate with the design and research team in problem-solving and help narrow down high-level wireframes and designs.

Stephanie shared an example of the NPR ONE app. At NPR, all shows, media, and content created were available to the listeners via different radio shows. To provide a differentiated offering, especially for the younger audience who are used to streaming content, NPR created an app by owning and consolidating their own content.

Stephanie was eager to talk with and observe how customers interact with NPR as well as other radio shows, but the NPR research department at that time was more geared toward broadcast; they did not truly support digital products. To get feedback on this new product idea, in addition to talking to the current NPR customers, Stephanie was also interested in engaging with a new audience to explore fresh new ideas and approach; She wanted public media fans who stream content either offline or online. As she explored options, Stephanie hoped she could recruit enough of the right participants for the tests to be meaningful.

Stephanie took an innovative approach and reached out to her customers where she knew she could find them - NPR's social channels. In a call out to her audience via NPR's Facebook and Twitter accounts, Stephanie filtered her target audience via a Facebook Survey based on criteria such as how the potential participants consume digital media content, where are they were listening from, their frustrations, and what they liked about these apps. Once she identified the right audience, she ran research sessions online. Stephanie's approach was different compared to the focus groups I have attended and conducted in the past. I normally meet with my participants in person. I was, therefore, curious to know how she executed the sessions and if the sessions were productive.

At these online research sessions, Stephanie shared, she led the team through multiple exercises:

- Individual questions where participants shared individual thoughts with just her.

- Group discussions where all participants posted thoughts to questions posted by Stephanie while interacting and responding to each other.

- Participants drew and posted pictures of how they expected this "perfect" app to look and function as well as shared screenshots of apps they like.

The online research sessions proved better than she had anticipated. Stephanie shares, "I remember one time I had about thirty people come for a Facebook event. And we spent time talking about curated listening lists. As we were asking questions we had, people were drawing and taking pictures and posting it on Facebook to the event page, while interacting with each other. It was brilliant!" The team walked from these sessions with key findings that they used to start building their prototype.

By lowering the barrier for participation, Stephanie and her team were not limited to the DC metro area where the NPR offices are located; instead, they were able to recruit participants from across the world. By recruiting the right audience who consumed digital media content versus traditional radio broadcast and getting more participants, the team was able to get additional data (user opinions), thereby increasing their confidence in making design decisions. Yet important was the fact that online events equalized the participants as sometimes in-person sessions are dominated by a few folks and their ideas, and not all participants are able to contribute equally.

This example of co-creating with your customers increases the chance of product success. The well-defined, organized, and moderated session helped NPR engage their target audience and create the resulting app, NPR One. The app is their radio app with curated news and stories from local and national public radio stations. NPR ONE was awarded Finalist in the 2015 Innovation by Design Awards.

If co-creating is not an option, you can follow Shlomo and Saurabh's example and test design options, or you can learn from Mileha—the user researcher and designer from the Netherlands—and repeatedly try and iterate with your customers. There are many options to test the design; however, all options start and end with our customers.

Blind Arrogance	Empathetic Arrogance
Design for the customer	Design with the customer

WAZE: COMBINING COMMUNITY AND DATA WITH AN AMAZING DESIGN

As we discuss designing with intent, I want to share yet another example of an app that brings all these key points together - user community, design, and data. Waze is a navigation app; think Google maps but with a twist. A community-based traffic and navigation app, Waze is powered and used by drivers all over the world. Drivers connect with one another and work together to improve each other's driving experience.

Ehud Shabtai, the founder of Waze, was born and brought up in Israel (Vashishtha 2019). He completed his undergraduate degree in Philosophy from Tel-Aviv University, followed by an MS degree in Computer Science from the same university. Shabtai's problem was that the GPS was insufficient to get him from place to place as it lacked real-time knowledge of traffic along the different routes. With a background in software engineering, he decided to develop a new application that would help people find the direction to various places, along with the traffic information along the route.

In 2006 Shabtai built an app named FreeMap Israel. The app included a database for the Israeli map and crowdsourced the information from speed cameras. In 2008, he partnered with Uri Levine and Amir Shinar to commercialize and launch the Waze app. Waze crowdsourced data—driver-sourced mapping, community curation, and citizen traffic reporting, all came together to add an interactive element to the user experience. Which not only quickly became addicting but also tended to be more accurate thanks to its obsessive army of reporters relaying traffic data and updates in real-time. In 2013, Google bought Waze.

The Waze team partnered with Pentagram, the global design agency, on the design refresh. In May 2021, the Pentagram website shared that Waze's global community comprised 130 million users in over 180 countries, who collectively joined their local voices to help beat traffic. An avid community of over 500,000 map editors also helped document route changes. In the article "Under the Hood: Behind the Brand Refresh," published in June 2020 on the Waze Medium channel, Jake Shaw, Head of Creative, shares the company's approach to the community-driven Waze design refresh. From regular meetups to quantitative studies, the strong Waze community actively participated in the process, sharing how they felt about the brand and what they expected. Discussions with nearly 13,000 participants made two things clear: bringing consistency and simplicity to the elements that have always been part of the brand and giving the community an opportunity to express themselves *through* the brand. These discoveries spanned throughout their app experience, as well as Waze's mission to make the travel journey fun.

The foundational element to the design is a grid that represents the "streetscape," the basis of the Waze app. The grid becomes busy and dynamic in the city and, conversely, open and expansive in the suburbs. The design grid can also be applied to any customer touchpoint—think email, social media, or the website.

When picking colors to represent the community, the designers stayed away from a clean, minimal, tech style of representation. They instead leaned toward bright, fun colors selected bright, vibrant colors that represent the very nature of the community. These colors fill the open spaces between the streets, roads, avenues and bring the app together in a unique and joyful way.

The community's desire to be able to represent themselves through the brand has been pulled through the refreshed Wazer symbol by defining Moods. Moods are used to reflect how drivers feel on the road. In the article, Shaw says, "We had a lot of fun exploring the range of emotions people feel out there. A dozen drivers could all feel different in the exact same situation, so we set about capturing as many of those feelings as possible. This was critical to us because the Moods act as a visual reminder of all of us out there working together. We want to represent all different types of people in all different moments on their journey and make people smile, even when there might not be much to smile about."

Pulling all the design elements together, the colorful grid-like maps overlaid with the drivers representing themselves through the Moods brings together this fun, vibrant and active community of Wazers. In May 2021, 2.7 million reviewers rated the app a solid 4.9 out of 5 on the App Store, whereas on the Google Play Store, 8 million-plus users rate it a 4.4 out of 5. When apps take their users into account and pay attention to how the users interact with their digital products, the experience becomes more profitable for both parties.

KEY TAKEAWAYS

As we shift to digital channels, user experience is key to building a strong relationship with our customer; after all, it is the only tangible part of the digital product that the user can see, touch, and hopefully feel.

In this chapter, we focused on the fact that experience design is more than a decorative garnish. Instead, it is about how the product works. It has the power to impact user behavior and turn our customers into our true brand fans. To accomplish this, we have to be intentional with our design; we have to be passionate and empathetic about what we are designing, immerse ourselves in understanding why we are building the product, and be clear on the objectives. Test, create, or co-create with your customer while tracking the customer behavior.

Blind Arrogance	Empathetic Arrogance
Design is the "pretty" element in a digital product	Design is the functional element in a digital product that spurs action
The product usage data meets our team objectives	The customer behavioral data helps us understand and improve the product experience
It is just the design. We have a great technical solution.	The broader one's understanding of the human experience, the better design we will have.
Design for the customer	Design with the customer

CHAPTER 9

Missionaries not Mercenaries

——

Do you remember the game of telephone that we played as children? Someone comes up with a phrase and whispers it to the person sitting next to them. The game continues until the last person in the game says the phrase aloud. The probability of this vocalization matching the initial phrase is low; generally, what emerges is a garbled version of the original message.

In the early days, the software development process followed a linear, sequential approach. Business stakeholders worked with business analysts to define and document what they wanted to build. The business analyst captured these in the form of written requirements. Business analysts then handed over the requirements for the user experience teams to design, who in turn passed on the designs and criteria for the technical teams to build. This method is called the "waterfall" approach because each phase of the project cascades into the next, following steadily down like a waterfall. You can equate the waterfall approach to the game of telephone. In the traditional waterfall development methods, developers are often shielded from businesspeople. They are told what to build. Additionally, once the requirements are handed off to the technical team, they are frozen or become unchangeable, so technical teams can provide a time and budget estimate for delivery. There is not much flexibility to change or update requirements without impacting the time and budget.

At a conference organized by Wharton business school in San Francisco in March 2000, John Doerr, the venture capitalist and chairman at Kleiner Perkins Caufield & Byers, spoke about the meaningful impact of great ventures. A blog post on the Wharton website dated April 13, 2020, captured Doerr's speech where he shared that truly great ventures are led by missionaries, not mercenaries. Doerr describes "missionaries" as the entrepreneurs who want to build companies to last, compared to "mercenaries," who want to establish companies primarily to flip them.

While the two might seem similar at first glance, they are, in fact, very different. "Mercenaries are driven by paranoia; missionaries are driven by passion," stated Doerr, "Mercenaries think opportunistically; missionaries think strategically. Mercenaries go for the sprint; missionaries go for the marathon. Mercenaries focus on their competitors and financial statements; missionaries focus on their customers and value statements. Mercenaries are bosses of wolf packs; missionaries are mentors or coaches of teams. Mercenaries worry about entitlements; missionaries are obsessed with making a contribution. Mercenaries are motivated by the lust for making money; missionaries, while recognizing the importance of money, are fundamentally driven by the desire to make meaning."

When I think of Doerr's thoughts on missionaries and combine them with Simon Sinek's view of the infinite game, in my mind, you need missionaries to be capable of playing an infinite game. Missionaries focus on the just cause and long-term goals; they do not dwell on the competition and short-term wins, as they are obsessed with outlasting the competition with strategic, long-term wins that make a meaningful impact.

You need missionaries to play an infinite game.

As we think of product teams, we need to think of products, marketers, designers, developers, and data scientists as collectively sitting at the same table in a missionary role. Each role is empowered to contribute to one just cause. Where I have seen teams fail is when they leave technologists off the table. Instead, developers are treated as mercenaries who are asked to focus on short-term goals and build what has already been decided and agreed upon by the business and experience teams. They are told to focus on the sprint rather than being asked to contribute to the marathon. They are asked to focus on an opportunity at hand rather than thinking strategically about the product's health. This approach to treat technical partners as mercenaries is blind arrogance and hurts the product in the long run.

Blind Arrogance	Empathetic Arrogance
Technical teams are mercenaries. They build the product based on specified requirements	Technical teams are missionaries. They are part of the product team and contribute to both product strategy and development

TECHNICAL TEAMS AS MERCENARIES

I specifically recollect a project that I supported in the early days. The business wanted to redesign the website's homepage to pull forward all the services the company provided on the homepage. In the first step of the process, a team of three business analysts interviewed and worked with the multiple key stakeholders across the company to capture what they wanted on the homepage. Each stakeholder wanted their offering showcased top and center. The requirements were complex, ran over several pages, and prioritized into high, medium, and low levels of importance. The business analysts then passed the baton to the second team—the designers—in order to commence the second step.

Designers came up with a layout that resembled a card layout; multiple cards on the homepage provided high-priority stakeholders the homepage real estate to make their splash. After the stakeholders approved the designs and functionality of the new homepage, the designers passed the baton, or the requirements, to the technical teams.

We were now at step three—almost six to eight months into the process—and the technical teams reviewed the requirements for the very first time. We held multiple requirement-review sessions. The technical teams came up with a timeline and a budget to implement the requirements. The business pushed back and asked the technical team to shorten the timeline and the cost. The technical teams asked the company to reduce the scope. The back-and-forth negotiations continued for another four to six weeks. Once the business and technical teams agreed to a revised scope, budget and timeline, the requirements were sent back to the business analyst and design teams to adjust and align with the new agreement between the business and technical teams. The third step was the most challenging and painful part of the process, as conflict and push-and-pull between teams ran rife. By now, we were at least ten months in, and there was bad blood between the business and technical teams over the negotiations.

With agreement on what was to be built, for what cost, and when the homepage would be delivered, the technical teams officially accepted the baton, and, as the fourth step, the development actually kicked off. While the business teams waited, we held weekly meetings with the technical teams to address any questions that the developers had. Now, six months into development and more than sixteen months from the start of the project, the technical teams shared a sandbox where the business finally started to see the design in reality. One of the business units had been dismantled since then, and we had to update designs and functionality to replace their homepage card with another service offering. Developers now pulled in the testers by sharing the baton with them. When the baton passed on to the testers, and the testing process kicked off (thus, beginning step six), we were more than eighteen months into the process. Marketing teams geared up and started the marketing efforts and the newly designed homepage launched, and the teams celebrated the hard work. It was more than double the time it took to birth a baby; but our baby was beautiful, and everyone loved it.

Three months into the new homepage, the teams realized how hard the homepage was to maintain. With weekly content updates and translation costs that the operations team was not staffed for, the maintenance costs were higher than anticipated. Secondly, the data showed us that the bounce rate increased as users were unable to find the services they were looking for—a hard price to pay for an effort that cost an arm and a leg and took more than eighteen months to build. Following that, whispers of yet another pending redesign could be heard in the hallways.

EMPOWERING TECHNICAL TEAMS TO BE MISSIONARIES

As seen in the example above, using the traditional "waterfall" development methodology hindered companies and teams from delivering value to the customers and negatively impacted the business from meeting market needs. On February 11, 2001, at The Lodge at Snowbird ski resort in the Wasatch mountains of Utah, seventeen software development thought leaders met to talk, ski, relax, and try to find common ground to succeed in the new economy. They aimed to aggressively expand into the era of e-business, e-commerce, and the web. They named themselves "The Agile Alliance" and agreed on the *Manifesto for Agile Software Development.*

The manifesto, at the core, is about delivering good products to customers by operating in an environment that does more than just talk about "people being our most important asset" but actually "acts" as if people are the most important part of a product's development. By focusing on the customer and reducing the emphasis on processes and documentation, the manifesto brought experience and technology teams, as well as the marketers, closer together. The goal of this cross-functional team is to create software products that add value to the customer and help businesses learn, pivot as needed, and grow. The Manifesto, as succinctly worded on the Agile manifesto website, is as follows:

"We are uncovering better ways of developing software by doing it and helping others do it. Through this work we have come to value:

Individuals and interactions over processes and tools.

Working software over comprehensive documentation.

Customer collaboration over contract negotiation.

Responding to change over following a plan.

That is, while there is value in the items on the right, we value the items on the left more."

The agile manifesto sets teams up to play an infinite game as collaborators. With the power to bring a team of missionaries—the business owner, product manager, project manager, designers, developers, data analyst/scientist, testers - on the same table, it removed the sequential process of handing requirements down to technical teams and, most importantly, the back-and-forth negotiations on what to build. Instead, the agile methodology empowered teams to think about what delivers the most value to the customer and business. Upon determining a potential answer, the methodology then encourages building and testing their solutions iteratively in small chunks so that it is easy to respond to market changes and what you learn from the customers. Involving the technical teams at the beginning increases the chance of building a more sustainable or maintainable solution.

In an agile methodology, the developers are missionaries—equally accountable and contributors as the rest of the team.

DOMAIN KNOWLEDGE IS IMPORTANT TO LEAD A MISSION

In Chapter 2, "Playing the Infinite Game," I reflected on Simon Sinek's emphasis on the "just cause" as a crucial factor toward playing the infinite game. We discussed how teams need to understand the mission and what customer problems we are trying to solve. In the examples above, we have seen how the industry pivoted to agile and pulled developers at the table to help deliver value faster. In this new role, developers are set up to be missionaries rather than mercenaries. But in order for missionaries to perform, it is essential that they have domain knowledge—namely, that they understand the ins and outs of the business.

To better understand the impact of domain knowledge on development, I spoke to Mark, a veteran technologist. In this career, Mark has worked at several federal agencies in different roles. As we reflected on how domain knowledge impacts technical teams, Mark detailed his time at the Virginia Hospital Center in the early 2000s.

Mark's job at the center was overseeing the technical infrastructure and security of the hardware and applications across the hospital. The machines and applications ranged from the software running on the nurse stations and front-desk offices to the devices found in the operation theater. As he went about his daily job, Mark often interacted with his "customers," the nurses and doctors, to better understand how they used the software applications as well as the machines during surgical procedures. The surgeons often complained that the systems *"gave them more information that they needed,"* especially during surgical procedures, and it hindered them from making critical decisions in a timely manner. The doctors and surgeons had worked with several medical technologists to solve the problem, but all had failed. They finally asked Mark for help.

For the next three months, Mark sat in about twenty open hearts surgeries. He sat nearby the patient's head and watched everybody work in the room. He noticed that the typical open-heart surgery requires at least two to three pairs of hands. As surgeons do not communicate with one another in open-heart surgeries, Mark spent a lot of time—both during and after the surgery—with circulating nurses, the perfusionist, the physiologist, or whoever was in the room to understand all the details. This included taking note of the different applications being used, alongside the varying patient data displayed on multiple screens in the operation theatre.

Armed with the working knowledge of the operation room, Mark started to simulate the room and how the machines could be better physically configured to make the operation room layout more effective. Mark explained that there was no computer-aided design back then, and it was not until ten years later that Autodesk Revit came out with similar technologies. To be nimble in his solution, Mark used Styrofoam and pipe cleaners to model and remodel the operating room and then invited surgeons to pretend to use the "machines." He continued to iterate until the surgeons agreed they got it right.

Next, Mark tackled what the surgeons complained about the most, that being "the systems with too much information." When observing the surgeons, Mark noticed that they had to switch from screen to screen to get the information they were looking for. As it was not instantaneous, the surgeons worried that the few seconds lag, in complicated situations, would adversely affect the patient.

Mark dove deeper to understand how patient health data was pulled across multiple applications; he worked across as many as ten applications to streamline and retrieve what surgeons qualified as the necessary amount of data on display. He then went one step further and created an early version of the voice recognition technology for common commands a surgeon uses during procedures, such as, "I want to see the Pulse Oximeter," and the system would pull it up on the screen. Mark explained, "This was the perfect marriage of information technology with medical knowledge from nurses and doctors. I learned that you can't be in the business, unless you understand the business. Every technology project is just a subset of a business project. "

In a 2018 article for *The International Journal of Advanced Computer Research* concerning the impact of domain knowledge when building requirements, authors Maria Latif, Toseef Aslam, and Palwashay Sehar concur with Mark's point of view. They argue that an accurate requirement is imperative for a successful project because projects are based on user needs. An in-depth understanding of the problem helps and improves the quality of project construction. They proceed to note that domain knowledge is a key factor in gathering requirements, understanding the problem, and the ease of project construction. Mark's story further validates this research. As a technologist, he would not be able to solve the surgeon's problem effectively and efficiently without observing them in the operation room, asking questions, and understanding their true needs.

In this example, Mark is out on a mission to simplify and improve the surgeon's experience while operating on a patient. Similarly, to ensure your technical partners are building a solution to the right problem, it is essential that they are at the table. I participated in a prioritization meeting that was attended only by business folks. When asked about their technical counterparts, I was told, "The product manager will explain the prioritized feature to the tech lead and come back with an estimate." This team took pride in the fact that they practiced agile. But with technical counterparts missing on the table, I do not call this an agile team.

Having technical expertise at the meeting would have helped the team have a holistic conversation about business priorities and how technical teams could help move them forward. The back-and-forth estimations reminded me of the "waterfall" approach. I cannot emphasize enough how much technology needs to be at the table for every conversation if you want to succeed. *Empathetic arrogance* means pulling your technical teams to the table. *Blind Arrogance* is when you think, "*I got this. I can explain it to my technical counterpart.*" Even with my technical degrees, I would rather have my technical team at the table and not play a game of telephone.

Blind Arrogance	Empathetic Arrogance
We are documenting requirements to share with our technical team. We are providing them with sufficient details so that they know what to build	We have our technical team at the table with us discussing product strategy and how we can build a humanistic product that turns our customers into true brand fans
Product requirements are sufficient for technical teams to build a great product	Domain knowledge is a must for technical teams to build a great product

TECHNOLOGY FOR A MISSION

In recent digital wars, companies are working to leverage large amounts of customer data to study patterns and identify gaps while also providing customers with real-time personalized experiences that are unique to each and every one of us. Artificial Intelligence (AI) is an arm of computer science that aims to replicate or simulate human intelligence in machines, so they are capable of performing tasks that typically require human intelligence. Many of these artificial intelligence applications are powered by machine learning, an application of AI that helps the application to automatically learn and improve from experience. AI applications differ from the natural intelligence displayed by humans, which involves consciousness and emotionality. Yet, Eno, a virtual assistant built by Capital One, a financial services company, comes pretty close to a human.

One day when checking email, I received an email from Capital One, my credit card and bank provider, with the subject line, "Were you double-charged?" Curious, I opened and read the email from Eno; it informed me about two identical charges I received for the same magazine. Earlier that day, I had purchased two separate gift subscriptions for my mom and sister. I was pleasantly surprised and delighted to learn that Capital One ensured that I was not double charged. What had typically been a chore to me—scouring through the monthly credit card bill to make certain that no fraudulent or inaccurate transactions appeared—was now being shared by Capital One. I saw this digital product as Capital One leveraging existing customer data to intentionally deepen and build a stronger relationship with its customers. Eno is an excellent example of leveraging and humanizing technology to benefit customers.

Later that year, I had the opportunity to attend an "Innovation Evening" organized at the Capital One Headquarters in McLean, Virginia. I was especially thrilled to hear the Head of Conversation Design speak about the team's approach to building Eno. During the talk, she discussed people's unconscious biases when talking about money. How comfortable are men with the idea of speaking to women about financial matters? Are they more likely to reach out to other men instead? Would women feel more comfortable discussing money with other women, or do they believe men to be more reputable when talking about money? To avoid building on any preconceived notions, the team intentionally decided to keep Eno gender neutral.

Intrigued by this level of detail, I read several blogs on the Capital One website. In a blog postdated September 29, 2017, I learned that Eno was designed by a team consisting of a journalist, a user experience designer, and an anthropologist. The process of building out Eno's holistic persona or a fictional character was led by a former filmmaker who had previously worked for studios such as DreamWorks and Pixar. To bring Eno's character or persona to life, this small and mighty team observed customers in order to understand how Eno can resonate emotionally with the customers. They visualized Eno's personality: "If Eno were human, it would move through space with confidence and a slight spring in its step. If you were sitting in the same space with Eno, it would pull up a chair and make itself comfortable, like it had all the time in the world to hear what you had to say." The mission to build this humanistic persona led to a methodology for creating Eno's language that began with the character design and philosophy behind who Eno is.

To create those responses and persona, the team worked to build the type of language Eno might use to respond to each specific question. At the same time, the language had to capture the relatable, empathetic nature of Eno so that customers feel like *they are talking to a trusted mentor, such as a favorite professor, teacher, or advisor,* for example. The user experience designer on the team helped create a visual identity and gave direction on how customers may interact with Eno, while the former journalist helped provide a structure to Eno's responses. The anthropologist's role pertained to incorporating customers' emotions and behaviors into Eno's design and providing an understanding of how people want to talk about their money via different channels.

In addition to powering Eno with a humanistic persona, the virtual assistant uses a natural language or machine language processing solution—the more people text and talk to the bot, the more it will understand and learn how to respond to customer questions. To build out Eno's functionality, the engineering team built a natural language processing solution that learned how to speak 'bank' with the customers. In a blog post published on the company's website in September 2018, the Head of Software Engineering shared that as financial institutions often have their own vocabulary, such as transaction, authorized user, fraudulent activity, but humans don't usually think in those terms, the team decided to build their own natural language processing (NLP) technology that deeply understands financial services terms while allowing them to deliver the best possible experience to their users.

The extended team working on Eno used real customer conversations from chat logs. They worked closely with customer service teams to analyze hundreds of thousands of web chats between customer service representatives and real customers. The machine learning engineers trained Eno on these conversations, building a rich and layered language model. For example, questions such as "Want to check your balance?" or "What's my balance?" or "What amount do I owe?" This natural language processing focused not only on how the chat bot might respond to certain queries but also on Eno's persona and the structured response framework built by the design team. Each customer interaction adds to Eno's language database, which, by proxy, allows the team to continually learn new things about how customers interact with Eno.

Eno is an example of how business, product, experience, and technical teams come together to build products that turn their customers into true brand fans. My interaction with Eno via email and messaging, as well as the evening in 2019 that I spent in the Capital One headquarters, made me want to work with these passionate teams on a mission to change banking for the better. I continued my conversations with the company, and, in early 2021—while still writing this book—I accepted an opportunity to join the product design team.

KEY TAKEAWAYS

If you leave this chapter with just one thing, let it be the fact that no digital product is complete without having technical teams at the table when thinking, strategizing, or building products. Furthermore, to build a product that shocks, surprises, and wins the hearts of your customers, it is essential to have representatives from all the four product components—marketing, experience design, technology, and data—at the table. If you want to build a great product, make sure you bring your technical partners along. The examples we explored in this chapter (specifically, the stories of Mark and Eno) drive home the point that equipping technical teams with domain knowledge empowers them to be true missionaries—and we need a team of missionaries in order to play the infinite game.

Blind Arrogance	Empathetic Arrogance
Technical teams are mercenaries. They build the product based on specified requirements	Technical teams are missionaries. They are part of the product team and contribute to both product strategy and development
Product requirements alone are sufficient enough for technical teams to build a great product	Domain knowledge is a must for technical teams to build a great product

CHAPTER 10

The Complete Data Story

———

I remember a time when an organization I worked for engaged a consulting company to advise us on our digital strategy. One of the key elements that emerged from the consultation was the slogan, "Data versus Opinion." This slogan propagated the mindset that teams and individuals leverage data to make a decision or get the point across instead of merely stating and pushing an opinion. This philosophy infiltrated the organization from the utmost top to the very bottom. All meetings started with dashboards; all conversations and decisions originated and ended around data. Data became king.

What makes the digital landscape unique, when compared with the non-digital channels, is that while we browse digital channels, we leave breadcrumbs behind throughout every action. Mindless to us, with the smartphones and smart devices around us, we produce a ton of human behavioral data. These behavioral data breadcrumbs collect information on the number of steps we walk, the flight of steps we climb, the hours we sleep, quality of our sleep, the route we drive on a daily basis, the time we spend in the car, the movies we watch, the temperature we set at home, the books we enjoy listening to, the things we buy, and so many more pieces of our daily lives. Our human data becomes abstract and represented by charts, bars, and graphs. When we pull these pieces of data together, the data tells a story about our daily routine. But the story will never be 100 percent accurate. Depending on what pieces of data we decide to pull together, we will get a different variation of our day. Therefore, while data is at the center of every part of our digital lives, it can also be biased and, as such, should not be considered objective.

And this lack of objectivity is exactly what happened within the organization. We all started to look at data as the means to an end. We got selective about using data that supported the story we wanted to tell. We focused on vanity metrics—metrics that made us look good, very much like the *Product Doomsday* team that touted the conversions but did not showcase the complete picture with the number of users who came and left the site without checking a single product.

To build digital products that grow our brand fanbase, we cannot cherry-pick the data to paint a partial customer story. Empathetic arrogance is when we use data to tell a complete account of our customer's journey and their experience with our product. Starting with this baseline helps us identify areas of opportunity to enhance our product and make our customers our true brand fans.

Blind Arrogance	Empathetic Arrogance
Focus on data snapshot that highlights team or product performance	Focus on event stream data that highlights the customer performance

VANITY METRICS VERSUS CLARITY METRICS

As product builders, we often get stuck up in performance metrics that make us look good as a team or company but do not help us improve products that offer value to our customers. In an exclusive interview with First Round, Lloyd Tabb, founder of Looker, now part of Google Cloud, shares the difference between *vanity metrics* (performance data that, as the word conveys, are pats on the back) versus *clarity metrics* (data indicators that provide direction so we can work on what delivers customer value). I equate these metrics to cause and effect. Once you know the cause, you are empowered to improve the product, thus resulting in happy brand fans.

Vanity metrics are the effect, but it is not until you look at the clarity metrics that you truly start to understand and diagnose the cause.

Lloyd defines these metrics as:

Vanity metrics are surface-level metrics. They're often large measures that impress others, like the number of downloads or the total number of users. These pieces of data could lead to many fortuitous business opportunities, such as initiating partnerships and gaining oneself a following.

Clarity metrics are operational metrics, like the number of minutes a day your product actually gets used or how long it took for a user to get service. These are the hidden gears that drive growth. Honing in on the clarity metrics to understand the cause and using them to improve the product can truly influence your competitive advantage.

In the interview, Lloyd says, "Vanity metrics aren't useless. They have their use case but are points of comparison for *other* people to evaluate you. Don't focus on them internally. Tracking clarity metrics builds great businesses."

The five tips below can help keep ourselves from getting seduced by vanity metrics and provide guidance on honing our instincts for real, productive measurement:

- Elevate metrics that predict the behavior of individual customers over time, not just capture a snapshot in aggregate for comparison with competitors.

Lloyd suggests that we zero in on the earliest act of service. An example, ride-sharing companies most often reference monthly active riders to measure performance. But that is the vanity metric as it does not explain why customers keep coming back or how services can improve. To make service better, Lloyd suggests measuring pickup times as the metric that measures service. The faster the car arrives, the more likely I am to use the service again. Lloyd says, "The difference between waiting one minute and ten minutes is a clear indicator of the quality of service. Analysis of the data will probably show you a cliff of what's acceptable in wait times. Tracking wait time failures across dimensions like neighborhood or driver will improve customer satisfaction and repeat business over time."

As you capture product data, make sure you identify metrics that help you measure the customer experience with why they are using your product. Yet another example of clarity metrics is the merchandising platform example we worked through in chapter eight, "Design with Intent," we broke down the clarity metrics into:

a. **Repeat Customer**: Noting the number of repeat customers to understand if customers come back.

b. **Product Category Views**: Browsing pattern across product categories to understand the popular categories and determine if categories at the bottom of the page saw any traffic.

c. **Customer Purchase Behavior with Focus on Discounted Items:** Customers purchasing a higher-priced item when an identical item was available at a lower price clearly indicates a faulty design (regulations required us not to suppress the lower priced item)

    d. **Browsing to Purchase Behavior:** Customers purchasing an item after browsing similar items in the category

- Organize your event stream to provide a chronological view of how people move through your product so you can test parts of it.

Companies typically bucket their users based on demographic attributes, product lines, or building their data into separate transactional tables. Separate tables are easier to read and make your software work. But they won't give you a comprehensive view of what's going on with your users through time. Therefore, rather than create data silos based on the company's internal products or customer attributes, organize data based on customer events or journeys.

Referring back to Chapter 8, we noticed that siloed data disguised real metrics. It was only when we strung the metrics together in a customer event string that we started to notice the problems. Lloyd suggests we centralize user activities and milestones into a single data stream. Event streams show how people move through your product and allow you to analyze their behavior.

- Don't fall into the A/B testing trap. Instead, call your customers when you spot a blip in their behavior. Data can't reveal how people feel.

At Looker, a data exploration and discovery business intelligence platform company that Lloyd founded, active engagement was the first metric he measured. How many active minutes did people spend in the software every day? "I didn't care about revenue or number of users. When we got a new client, I needed to know whether they were *actually using* the software," he states, "It's easy for vanity metrics to misguide companies. One can boast that 90 percent of a customer's employees have logins, but how many people actually use it? If they do use it, are they navigating through it actively or just leaving it on in the background? It's the same story with number of accounts. It doesn't tell you *how* people use your product. Sometimes, you even have to call them and find out."

He also cautions against overusing A/B testing, especially if your data is siloed. Lloyd says that any graphics changes will not yield accurate results if your data is siloed. Even if the difference in a button dimension or color produced more clicks, it is not until you combine that with the conversion or purchase data that you start to understand the effectiveness of the test. Instead, he recommends studying a customer's event streams and calling individual people. Every time Lloyd finds an outlier in Looker's userbase, he looks up the customer's contact information and calls. During the early years, he did this daily. "I call people because I want to know how they feel using our software. If they aren't using Looker, I want to know why. Is there something wrong? Are they stuck? If they are active users, I want to understand their experience and how we can improve it," says Lloyd.

- Make sure every department understands their failure rate and is equipped to decrease it. Your logistics are key levers of your business.

A "failure rate" is the number of times your company is unable to deliver on its promise. This rate is a shared operational metric for all businesses—not just security. "To get the failure rates for your company, find them in *each* department first. Every function will have a different failure rate to assess their work. For customer experience (CX), it's how many times a CX rep fails to solve a customer problem. For supply chain, it's how many times do customers try to purchase a sold-out item," detailed Lloyd. "Every team member needs to know and monitor the failure rate for their specific role and department. Every time you change your process or product, the measure of your failure rates need to be adjusted."

Lloyd shares an example of how Venmo, the mobile payments company, once made a design change that made it easy for users to accidentally send money when they meant to request it. On the one hand, this drove vanity metrics, like a number of transactions, because each mistaken money transfer needed an extra one to counteract it. Venmo noticed the increased transactions and gleamed from the transaction pairs—a payment and a "reversal" that mirrored that transaction—if the new design was the cause. The team's hypothesis was correct, and they solved the problem by changing the design

- Teach your team how to siphon and see data. You need a team of data detectives, not a single Sherlock.

As data is part of every digital product, data fluency is not just for tech anymore. Every department in every company must invest in it: customer support, design, business development. Everyone should review and parse data to understand and identify anomalies. When they find an outlier, they've got to be ready to dive in. Lloyd says, "You can't scale if there's a line outside your data team's door."

In a recent role, everyone on the team trained on viewing customized Tableau dashboards in a way that told the complete story of the customer journey. A small, lean product team with everyone from product manager, markers, project and program managers, and developers learned to read and understand the data. It was helpful for each one of us to know how the product performance impacted our functions. Product marketers learned which campaigns and messaging were impactful. Product managers learned to view data and prioritize features. Project and program managers discovered the interdependency of data across products, and the team collectively learned how messaging on social media can be used to not only educate and inform but also transact. And, most importantly, the teams learned the importance of vanity versus clarity metrics. We learned to share the story across the organization; even when our vanity metrics did not look stellar, we always reported the cause and shared the plan to amend, thus building trust across the organization. We spoke to our customers and came back with qualitative data that helped us better understand the "why" behind our Tableau dashboards. This use of both qualitative and quantitative data helped us improve our products.

Blind Arrogance	Empathetic Arrogance
Lean on vanity metrics or feel-good metrics that tout team performance	Lean on clarity metrics to improve product performance, thus positively impacting vanity metrics

THE POWER OF SMALL DATA

LEGO, the toy brand, reminds me of childhood, creativity, and long hours of fun. These interlocking plastic blocks have entertained generations of kids. With the world moving toward the digital landscape in the 1990s, entertainment products also started shifting their focus to computers, handhelds, and videogames. In line with industry trends, LEGO diversified its portfolio and began moving away from the sole focus on building blocks and began expanding into theme parks, children's clothing, video games, books, and retail stores. They also manufactured bigger LEGO blocks. In spite of these well-thought-out moves, the international toy manufacturer was on the brink of bankruptcy. (Robertson and Breen 2014)

In his book, *Small Data: The Tiny Clues That Uncover Huge Trends,* published in 2016, Martin Lindstrom shares the story of how he used small human clues—which he refers to as "Small Data"—to revive LEGO. Lindstrom is the founder and chairman of Lindstrom Company, the world's leading brand & culture transformation group, operating across five continents and more than thirty countries. The company's goal is to place the customer at the center of everything and help reconstruct companies by focusing on customer needs. Martin has spent time with 2,000 families in over seventy-seven countries to get clues to how they live—resulting in the acquisition of what he likes to call Small Data. In his book, Lindstrom argues that Small Data explains the "why" behind what Big Data reveals.

During its transformation, every Big Data study LEGO commissioned to plan ahead drew the exact same conclusions: Future generations lacked the time and patience for LEGO. This generation's need for instant gratification would quickly run out of ideas and storylines to build and play. It was in the midst of constantly dipping LEGO market share that an ethnographic visit to the home of an eleven-year-old boy finally turned things around. On this day, the executives realized that everything they heard and knew about late twentieth and early twenty-first century children, their new digital behavior, and their need for instantaneous results were wrong.

The marketers visited an eleven-year-old boy in a midsize German city to find out if the LEGO consumer really was the same consumer as the one described by big data. They visited this boy to ask one simple question: "*What are you most proud of*?" The kid paused for a second and then pointed at an old pair of worn-down Adidas sneakers standing on the shelf. As he took those smelly shoes down from the shelf, the team, surprised, asked, "*Why*?" For this boy, the answer was obvious: "*Because they are my evidence, my trophy, to show I'm the best skater in town.*"

When you skate, you slide down the board, which creates a unique mark at a precise right angle on the shoes. The entire look of the sneakers and the impression they conveyed to the world was perfect. The shoes signaled to the world that he was one of the best skateboarders in the city. At that precise moment, LEGO realized with the utmost certainty that they were going about things in the wrong way. They understood that LEGOs give kids an opportunity to build on their imagination and become storytellers. If they could cultivate a similar sense of pride in children for mastering the art of building with blocks, the children will have all the time in the world to pay with bricks.

Big Data was telling LEGO that they needed to dumb down their product, but the visit to this eleven-year-old boy convinced them that they actually made their product more complex and challenging. Back in the office, they reengineered the brick to the standard size and, in contrast to their initial mindset, placed even smaller intricate bricks inside their toy sets. The bricks became more detailed. The instruction manuals became more complex and the construction challenging yet fun. Ten years later, during the first half of 2014, LEGO sales rose 11 percent to exceed two billion dollars. For the first time ever, LEGO surpassed Mattel. LEGO's story is a brilliant example of the use of Small Data.

Blind arrogance is when you blindly follow either Big or Small Data

without validating the hypothesis.

THE PULL OF BIG DATA

"Big Data" refers to the massive volume of behavioral bread-crumbs left behind by the billions of humans on the planet with access to digital products yet still continues to grow exponentially with time. This huge collection of information gives us the power to study patterns, identify gaps, enable us to provide our customers with real-time personalized experiences that are unique to each and every one of us. In Chapter 9, "Missionaries not Mercenaries," through Eno's example, we saw how companies are looking at their data with a new lens to simulate human intelligence in machines, so they are capable of performing tasks that typically require human intelligence. As the data grows, these applications automatically learn and improve from experience. Big Data analytics helps organizations harness their data and use it to identify new opportunities. That, in turn, leads to smarter business moves, more efficient operations, higher profits, and happier customers.

Let's talk about how our old friend, Waze, is using Big Data to transform the world. In Chapter 8, "Design with Intent," we discussed Waze as an app that combines community and data with a fantastic design. Waze is a community-based traffic and navigation app powered and used by drivers worldwide. The statistics that we reviewed earlier show how 130 million users in over 180 countries collectively connect to one another and share personal real-time traffic data to improve each other's driving experience. An avid community of over 500,000 map editors also helps document route changes. The unique process uses digital information in a clever and revolutionary way:

- Wazers drive with the Waze app open on their smartphones. The app collects navigational data transmitted in real-time to Waze, and an initial map is drawn.

- Wazers use the design feature *"Moods"* to convey how they are feeling on the roads as they drive. Accidents, potholes, traffic backups, and clear roads are some of the emotional data indicators sent to further improve the navigation data.

- As more data is collected, the map is made more accurate. For example, speed, direction, number of cars, etc., can be used to determine if a road is a highway, one-way, or a side street, after which traffic patterns are identified.

- Community members and map editors alter the map, add street names, correct inaccurate roads, etc.

Waze has created a virtuous cycle with positive network effects: more Wazers provide better data, better data leads to the creation of better maps, and better maps attract new Wazers. Waze helps us navigate traffic and save precious time.

This data also powers the Waze Connected Citizens Program (CCP). The Waze website describes the CCP program as key to bringing cities and citizens together to answer the questions "What's happening, and where?" Launched in October 2014 with ten city partners, the program has now expanded to 450 partners, including city, state, and country government agencies, alongside nonprofits and first responders, to name a few. CCP is symbiotic in nature, with Waze providing partners real-time, anonymous, proprietary incident and slow-down information directly from the drivers themselves. The partners, in turn, give Waze real-time information in advance surrounding government-reported construction, car accidents, and road closure data. CCP yields more data giving Wazers a greater ability to circumvent road closures and traffic jams. Cities, states, and countries make further use of the data to improve city planning, inform infrastructure decisions and increase the efficiency of day-to-day operations.

A great example of the use of Waze data is how the officials in Rio De Janerio analyzed traffic and incident data from Waze to identify neighborhoods that experience the most congestion on election days. Insights from this analysis were used during a secondary election to test transit management personnel staffing within communities.

SMALL DATA VERSUS BIG DATA

In the examples above, the use of small data in the LEGO story tells us the why while Waze big data is helpful to identify patterns that improve the real-time navigation experience for its customers and partners.

Given the power of both Small & Big Data, how do we use one or both to improve our digital products? In the Knowledge@

Wharton podcast, where Martin discusses his book, *Small Data*, he shares a brilliant example that illustrates the tension between Big Data (quantitative) and Small Data (qualitative). We see big companies such as Amazon that are thriving on Big Data, but we also see that Amazon has also opened several brick-and-mortar stores. Martin speculates that the book sales are flattening, and so are the Kindle sales. So, Amazon's Big Data is telling them that they need physical interaction. He connects the dots with something he learned when he delivered a keynote at the American Bookseller Association (ABA) in Denver. As he spoke to these independent booksellers across the world, he asked them, "Aren't you afraid of Amazon?"

They all said exactly the same, "No way, and I'll tell you why. Because they do not embed themselves into the community."

He shares that every bookstore today is embedding itself into the community by talking with authors. He discovered a bookstore with ten staff members that are running more than 1,000 book events a year. Big Data on the internet is good at going down the transaction path if you click, pick, and run. In contrast, Small Data is fueling the experiential shopping, the feeling of community, the sensory elements—all that stuff you can't replicate online.

In the podcast, Martin says, "I think it's fair to say if you take the top 100 biggest innovations of our time, perhaps around 60 percent to 65 percent are really based on Small Data. The issue here is that as we become so obsessed with Big Data, we forget about the creativity. You have to remember that Big Data is all about analyzing the past, but it has nothing to do with the future. You need the hypothesis first before you start to mine it and find correlations. "(Lindstorm, 2016)

My experience when working with Big Data and Small Data has been similar to Martin's story. In Chapter 8, "Design with Intent," we looked in-depth at the merchandising platform example in the story *"When Design Is the Problem."* While Big Data helped us understand our customer journey on the online marketplace and helped us identify gaps, we went back to the field to speak with our customers, who helped us understand the why behind their behavior. My experience has taught me that Big Data will help you see the breadcrumb trail detailing your customers' actions within the digital landscape. But to comprehend the "why" of it all, you will need Small Data, as that will help you understand humans— your customers.

KEY TAKEAWAYS

The data we collect in the "empathy" part of the book is the Small Data. Or, as Martin puts it, the "emotional DNA" we leave behind ourselves in the seemingly insignificant observations everything from how you place your shoes to how you hang your paintings.

In the "Arrogance" part of the book, we focused on Big Data to understand trends as we start to build a product. But regardless of how we use the data, the goal is to humanize it, as digital products are meant to solve a human problem and create an emotional connection with humans.

As we build digital products, the goal is not to use vanity metrics to feel good about ourselves but rather to lean on clarity metrics that help us understand how our digital products are working for our customers. When we positively impact the clarity metrics, we influence the vanity metrics as well.

Blind Arrogance	Empathetic Arrogance
Focus on data snapshots that highlight team or product performance	Focus on event stream data that highlight the customer performance
Lean on vanity metrics or feel-good metrics that tout team performance	Lean on clarity metrics to improve product performance, thus positively impacting vanity metrics
Big Data is the new gold for building digital products	We need both big and small data to build strong digital products. While Big Data tells us the "what," Small Data tells us the "why."

Data is a part of digital products at every step of the way—from conception to marketing to understanding product performance. Whether you leverage Small Data by listening to your customer or picking up the phone to call and talk to them, or use Big Data to create a single image of your customer, segment the data to market to the customer, or even use Big Data to create an AI product, you need data to power your product. If you were to equate a digital product with a car, then data is the fuel that drives it. Data is definitely a much-needed fourth component—alongside business, design, and technology—to build strong digital products. Without data, we cannot create them.

.

PART IV

LOOKING AHEAD

SURVIVING AND THRIVING IN A WORLD OF DIGITAL DARWINISM

The digital landscape continues to evolve, as does the art and science of building products. In Chapter 1, "Digital Darwinism," we saw how digital products have evolved from technology to customer experience, to marketing and business models, and now data. We also noticed that digital products decreased the barrier to entry in new markets, as most ideas can be copied, tweaked, and scaled. In this unfamiliar terrain, where products continue to evolve and competitors can easily threaten your existence, how do we play an infinite game where the fundamental rule is to outlast our competition?

In Part II, we learned how to be customer-focused and lean on empathic arrogance. Being *"good"* is not enough. We learned to first define what is essential and elemental to our customers and then scale it to win their hearts and minds.

We also explored customer obsession via listening and observing, especially if we want to scale to global markets, as each global market has its own nuances. In Part III, we built upon Part II by investigating the common pitfalls on the four components of a digital product—business insights with a focus on marketing, user experience design, technology, and last but not least, *data*.

In this section, we will build upon what we have learned and further explore how we can lean on one or more of these product components, as well as customer obsession, to create a competitive advantage.

CHAPTER 11

Determining Your Competitive Advantage

———

We are in an era of digital Darwinism where the critical element to survival is to play an infinite game and outlast your competition. In Chapter 2, Playing the Infinite Game, we learned the first rule to playing the infinite game is being clear on the just cause or the mission. A clear understanding of your just cause will ensure you serve your customer while building the ideal future in mind. Similarly, in his book, *The Five Most Important Questions You Will Ever Ask About Your Organization,* published in 1993, management guru Peter Drucker shares that the first and most important question for any organization is: "What *is our mis*sion?" Drucker writes, "The effective mission statement is short and sharply focused. It should fit on a T-shirt. It must be clear, and it must inspire. Every board member, volunteer, and staff person should be able to see the mission and say, 'Yes. This is something I want to be remembered for.'"

A clear mission or vision gives an organization the much-needed platform to build upon as the key differentiator.

Every digital product anchors itself to the company's mission in some capacity. For each product team, it is important to understand why we exist and what customer problems we are trying to solve. Obtaining and maintaining clarity of what the mission entails helps us identify our customers and understand what they value the most. After we have a sound understanding of our fundamentals, we can then move on to build digital products that meet and exceed our customers' needs. So, if our company's mission is the same as our competitor's, how do we differentiate ourselves? Especially seeing as the barrier to entry for the digital landscape is low, how do we make sure we can establish and retain a competitive edge? How do we stay relevant in an infinite game? In this chapter, we will explore how companies leverage the key components of a digital product as well as the mindset required to effectively build a barrier to entry.

CUSTOMER OBSESSION AS COMPETITIVE ADVANTAGE

Stealing or copying an idea or what is commonly called "idea theft" or "clone" is common among digital start-ups. As the concept has already been proven by the idea originator, a clone can be faster to scale than the original, seeing as they do not require any research or development time.

Shortly after Airbnb grew in the United States, they fell prey to idea theft in 2011. In the article "Airbnb Freaks Out Over Samwer Clones" for TechCrunch, Alexia Tsotsis reports an email that Airbnb sent to over one hundred thousand hosts, warning them about "impostor websites, like 9flats, Wimdu and Airizu. Additionally, Alexia speculates that Airbnb may be feeling threatened by these Airbnb clones created by the German Samwer brothers, who operate by creating European clones of existing high-profile US web companies. Her speculation was warranted, especially given the fact that the Samwers sold their eBay clone Alando.de to eBay in 1999 and their Groupon clone CityDeal to Groupon itself for around a hundred million Euros in 2010 (Tsotsis 2011). Fortunately, we already know that this story ends on a happy note, one where Airbnb comes out on top and continues to prevail, thrive, and even go public in late 2020. So, this begs the question: How did Airbnb manage to outsmart the Samwer brothers?

A 2015 video captures Brian Chesky, the co-founder of Airbnb, talking to Reid Hoffman about the challenges of scale at a Stanford Blitzscaling class, Brian shares how they scaled at a considerable speed to claim market dominance. He shares that while Airbnb had raised seven million dollars from Reid, by April 2010, the Samwer brothers had raised ninety million dollars. Airbnb took two and a half years to build a forty-person team, whereas they heard that the Samwer brothers had four hundred employees. The Airbnb co-founders were stumped! They had no idea how to open a second office while the Samwer brothers had opened twenty offices. Brian shares the dilemma, "Now the problem is that most companies that lose Europe, are just a smaller company; it is almost like a phone without email or phone without signal. There is no reason for it to exist. And we didn't know what to do. We had a proposition to buy the company, but it would have been very expensive, but more importantly, it would have been a huge cost culturally, and I didn't know what to do."

Brian recollects calling Mark Zuckerberg, the founder of Facebook, because the Samwer brothers had also cloned Facebook. Zuckerberg advised Brian not to buy or sell and that whoever has the best product will win this. Paul Graham, cofounder of start-up accelerator and seed capital firm Y Combinator, counseled Brian to basically pretend that the Samwer brothers had this baby that they did not want to raise. Brian thought, "We are founders; we want to grow this company, so I'm like a parent, and I want this child to grow into this wonderful company." Therefore, the most significant punishment Brian could conjure up for the brothers was to make them run this company for the long term.

Samwer brothers wanted to sell the company, but now they were stuck with running it, or as Brian suggested, "Raise the child that stuck with them for eighteen years." At that point, Brian knew the brothers would last for maybe a year, but they could not win in the long term, and that was the Airbnb strategy; They built a company long-term and ultimately won the game. Airbnb founders understood their Airbnb community in great detail, while the brothers could not understand their community. The customer advantage was with the Airbnb founders.

Brian and his cofounders ended up flying to Europe, hiring some country managers, and then taking them back to San Francisco, where they would be trained over the next couple of months. Following their training period, the managers were then tasked with flying home, hiring, and growing their teams. Brian and his co-founders opened eight to ten offices in three months and hired hundreds of people. Brian admits, "The Samwers gave us a gift. They forced us to scale faster than we ever would have." By choosing to grow at a breakneck pace, Airbnb has achieved a dominant position in its market.

This Airbnb story reiterates the importance of customer obsession as a differentiator. It takes passion in order to build and scale a customer base. This story also explains the importance of scale to play an infinite game. The positive outcome from this experience was that Airbnb scaled to Europe much faster than they had planned or expected.

Blind Arrogance	Empathetic Arrogance
Think like mercenaries who want to build companies to flip	Think like missionaries who want to build companies to last
Focus on an existing business model to scale	Focus on the customer to build a unique value proposition that can scale

DATA AS COMPETITIVE ADVANTAGE

In Chapter 10, "The Complete Data Story," we saw how companies are looking at their data to simulate human intelligence in machines, so they are capable of performing tasks that typically require human intelligence. What happens when two companies have a similar customer base and collect almost identical customer data? How can data be a differentiator?

With big data a current buzzword, many executives assume that the more customer data they capture, the more intelligent their machine learning tools become and the bigger their competitive advantage grows. But this is not always the case. Take, for example, the apps Pandora and Spotify. Both apps enable users to stream music—and the more songs you listen to, the more data the company gets, and thus, the better the personalized recommendations.

When Pandora debuted in 2005, it revolutionized the music industry. Pandora believes that everyone has a very personal relationship with music. Foundational to Pandora is its "Music Genome Project." Pandora's website details that a team of trained musicologists listened to, identified, and classified each song using as many as four hundred and fifty pre-determined musical attributes—each of which was then given a numerical value. Pandora uses these scores to determine song matches, thus providing a highly personalized listening experience to approximately seventy million users each month. Pandora's proprietary data-based Music Genome Project is hard to copy or build, thus offering a competitive advantage.

When you download and set up the Pandora app, users are asked for their age, gender, and zip code. The taxonomy behind the Music Genome Project uses these three pieces of data to understand customer preferences better and, as a result, create models. In a 2019 article for *Forbes*, Pandora's Vice President of Data Science, Oscar Celma, said, "We treat every individual very specially, and focus on contextual recommendations to understand what you like, what you listen to. We know barely anything about you, so let's give you something that people listened to in this age range or location." As he puts it, the thumbs-up and thumbs-down functions, which allow users to tell Pandora what they like or what they never want to hear again, "are the strongest explicit signal we have." But the implicit feedback is based on which songs users skip, either in full or in part, while replays reinforce how much someone likes a specific song even more than a thumbs-up. Pandora learns listening patterns and habits during different times of the day and how user behavior differs between weekdays and weekends. The app also tracks behavior to learn if a user is popularity-biased and listens to mainly Top 40, or prefers more obscure music, so it can play something the user has never heard before.

Spotify made its debut in 2008, which meant that Pandora had a three-year data lead on Spotify. However, today, Spotify is the world's most popular audio streaming subscription service. Based on data listed on its website, Spotify currently has three hundred and twenty million users, including one hundred and forty-four million subscribers, across ninety-two markets. How did Spotify overtake Pandora?

Both Pandora and Spotify enable their users to connect with friends, share their favorite songs, or recommend artists and playlists. However, these streaming clients differ vastly when it comes to comparing the social components of each service. In a February 2020 article for *Harvard Business Review*, Andrei Hagiu and Julian Wright explain that while Pandora users have the ability to share their favorite stations across Facebook and Twitter, it does not allow for data growth because on-demand playback is a paid service. Spotify allows users with numerous options to share individual songs, entire playlists, and even specific artists with any of their friends and followers on any app you can send a regular old text link to. What makes a data network grow is when the information learned from one customer translates into a better experience for another. Or the learning can be incorporated via a direct feature integrated visibly into the product or application. Users prefer to join more extensive networks as they have more people to interact with, which, in turn, generates more insights for the company.

As per the investor information on the Sirius XM website in May 2021, Pandora was acquired by Sirius XM for $3.5 billion in February 2019, whereas on the Reuter's website, Barry McCarthy, finance chief of Spotify, shares that Spotify went public and as of early November 2019 was worth $26 billion. Clearly, customization or personalization based on learning from an individual user's data helps keep existing customers locked in, but it doesn't lead to the type of exponential growth that network effects produce.

Yet another excellent example of an app that creates data network effects is our old friend, Waze. The navigation app builds on the mission to help people create local driving communities that work together to improve the quality of everyone's daily driving. James Currier, a Partner at NFX, a seed-stage venture firm headquartered in San Francisco, explains how Waze creates data network effects in a blog post titled *"What makes data valuable."* With Waze, the app automatically captures data from its users, which means that the app is getting smarter even as you sleep. The additional traffic conditions data that are shared by drivers instantly improves the experience for other users. For example, if I notice an accident on a busy highway and report it, it enhances the driving experience for another driver who may decide to take an alternate route. Additional data improves the product value of the app. Customers instantly see the value the app offers and pick it between other products.

The Waze app needs a minimum threshold of data before it starts to provide value. This minimum threshold hinders other competitors from entering this space. And most importantly, because of the real-time nature of the service, the data value does not become redundant, thus making it hard for competitors to provide the same value without a similar-sized userbase.

As you build digital products, explore features that enable you to grow your customer network while providing your customer value from said network. Think with a community mindset rather than creating a walled garden of data. In Chapter 10, "The Complete Data Story," we observed and discussed how Waze is sharing data with cities, states, and countries to create mutual symbiotic relationships that support one another while working with the greater good in mind.

Blind Arrogance	Empathetic Arrogance
Creates a walled garden of data that provides the customer with a great personalized experience but refrains the customer from benefiting from others	Creates a community of data that gets richer as we sleep. Each customer's data contributes toward improving the experience for other customers

TECHNOLOGY AS COMPETITIVE ADVANTAGE

It is hard to think of technology as a competitive differentiator, especially since most technology can be recreated. However, getting a lead in the technology space helps you build an advantage, as Amazon has shown via its cloud computation software, Amazon Web Services (AWS).

If you were a company and needed servers in a traditional digital model, you would either invest in a data center or in-house servers. The servers will need ongoing updates and maintenance. When you decide to scale your application(s), the backend infrastructure may need to be updated or scaled as well. AWS, the pioneer in cloud computing, disrupted the global business landscape by introducing a new way to manage computation.

In a 2015 interview with John Furrier and Dave Vellante, Founders of SiliconANGLE Media Inc, Andy Jassy, head of AWS, shared the background of AWS creation. "When we wrote the business plan for AWS, I don't think any of us had the audacity to predict that it would become this big this fast," Jassy recalls. But getting that big that fast is exactly what happened with AWS, and it shook up the entire technology industry.

In the interview, Jassy shares that as Amazon tried to scale, they kept bumping into one particular problem of accurately forecasting the time it took to complete both internal and external projects—a pattern that is very familiar across most digital developmental projects. Even when using the "agile" methodology, where you time-box the work to be delivered, you do not have an exact idea of what is produced and when. Agile improves the forecasting capability but does not guarantee it. At Amazon, the applications engineers and networking engineers spent way too much time building the same old infrastructure—storage and database solutions—over and over again. One product development lead after another pointed the finger at infrastructure development as their biggest pain point.

Amazon began hearing the same frustrations from external partners and CEOs around infrastructure services as a top priority. It was too expensive, hard to manage, required too much commitment, and was riddled with pricey upgrades. As the internet grew and companies started to scale, they realized the nuances of how much hardware was needed and the need to constantly update servers to maintain a global online presence.

In the end, Jassy says, AWS changed the way Amazon thought about development. They wanted to build in a service-oriented architecture, where all of their services were available in well-documented APIs so that anybody could use them. They also separated data from the presentation layer under the assumption that their merchants, selling physical products on the Amazon digital marketplace, would be able to leverage the data more effectively than Amazon would ever have the time to do itself. And that's just what happened. The AWS customers who used the new API increased conversion rates on their websites by nearly 30 percent.

As Amazon built data centers for themselves, it soon became apparent that every company was going to want this capability. And once AWS was launched, companies and developers flocked to AWS without any marketing. In the December 2020 HBR article "How Amazon thinks of Competition," based on Jeff Bezos' book *Invent and Wander: The Collected Writings of Jeff Bezos;* Bezos quotes, "When I launched Amazon.com in 1995, Barnes & Noble then launched Barnesandnoble.com and entered the market two years later in 1997. Two years later is very typical if you invent something new. We launched Kindle; Barnes & Noble launched Nook two years later. We launched Echo; Google launched Google Home two years later. When you pioneer, if you're lucky, you get a two-year head start. Nobody gets a seven-year head start (as Amazon did with AWS); I think that the big, established enterprise software companies did not see Amazon as a credible enterprise software company, so we had this long runway to build this incredible, feature-rich product and service that is just so far ahead, and the team doesn't let up."

According to February 2021 estimates from Synergy Research Group, Amazon's market share in the worldwide cloud infrastructure market amounted to 32 percent in the fourth quarter of 2020, still exceeding the combined market share of its two largest competitors, Microsoft and Google.

AWS has definitely provided Amazon with yet another competitive advantage. Though AWS is a technological advantage, its genesis came from Amazon's customer obsession to deliver better, faster service to their customers. This also builds on Amazon's mission to be the most customer-centric company on the planet. This example shows how customer obsession can provide opportunities in manners we do not think are possible.

CUSTOMER LOYALTY AS COMPETITIVE ADVANTAGE
In chapter three, "Framing the Problem," I talk about Marriott's growth to become the World's Largest Hotel Company. Before acquiring Starwood, Marriott had two loyalty programs, The Marriott Rewards and The Ritz-Carlton Rewards. I had the opportunity to digitally build and launch The Ritz-Carlton Rewards program with my colleague and friend, Kyle. After acquiring Starwood, Marriott combined the Starwood Preferred Guest (SPG) program with the two Marriott Loyalty Programs to form *Bonvoy*. This 120 million members strong loyalty program gives its members the flexibility to earn and redeem stays across an extraordinary portfolio of thirty hotel brands around the globe.

A September 2018 article "Four Competitive Advantages Marriott International Wants Shareholders to Grasp," captures four significant competitive advantages that CEO Arne Sorenson described during the company's second-quarter

2018 earnings conference call in early August. In the article, the author Asit Sharma, a Motley Fool analyst shares that the first and foremost is the extensive loyalty program, Bonvoy.

The second advantage is its new massive scale. As Arne shares, "With over 6,700 properties, we are positioned to take care of guests, whether they are on a Midwest road trip, making a sales call in Johannesburg, or enjoying a luxury resort getaway in the South Pacific. This growing breadth of product, and the growing number of earning and redemption opportunities, increases the value of our loyalty program, as guests don't need to look further than our properties virtually anywhere they may travel."

The third is the luxury properties that are part of the portfolio: "A loyalty program with significant luxury destinations and experiences is magnetic. Dreams about luxury Hawaiian holidays are motivating, particularly for travelers who spend a meaningful part of their lives on the road. In 2017, the 477 properties in our seven luxury brands represented just 9 percent of our rooms worldwide, but 17 percent of our loyalty-point redemptions."

The proprietary booking channels, providing guests the option to book in any medium of preference. "Like loyalty and luxury, our booking engines are also a significant competitive advantage. Guests can book our hotels directly through our websites, apps, call centers, [or] group sales offices, or on property."

I had an opportunity to talk to Julius Lai, a former data scientist for Marriott Rewards and The Ritz Carlton Rewards programs, currently serving as the Chief Product and Experience Officer for H&R block. In his previous roles, Julius was a data scientist supporting the Marriott loyalty programs, even before the word "data scientist" was coined. He later went on to assist Expedia, an online travel agency (OTA), as their Senior Director for Loyalty Marketing. As we discussed the different business models for the two companies, Julius shared his hypothesis, "For the specific case of Expedia, my hypothesis was that I had an opportunity to help a technology company that was new to loyalty, build loyalty in a meaningful way; this is different from a hospitality company, which was really good at technology running a loyalty program which at a time was thirty to thirty-five years old."

Marriott succeeded primarily because of its loyal member base and because its guests would visit, again and again, sometimes every year repeating. I saw the data supporting this when I worked with the information Julius pulled for us to build digital campaigns with the Marriott Rewards marketing teams. But what I had not realized until I spoke with Julius was the fact that though both companies targeted travelers, the Expedia customer base were deal seekers; a majority of customers never had more than two transactions with Expedia. So, the only way Expedia could win was by using staggering costs of money for acquisition costs.

Expedia could never compete with Marriott on its loyal customer base. This is Marriott's competitive advantage. By continuing to scale via acquisition but never losing focus on its loyal customer base Marriott has built a solid competitive advantage in the hospitality industry.

SCALE AND NIMBLENESS AS COMPETITIVE ADVANTAGE

In the examples above, Airbnb, Waze, Spotify, and Marriott—all have a common scale factor. Airbnb was able to scale to Europe after the incident with the Samwer brothers. Spotify's scale of data as compared to Pandora gave it an advantage. Waze's scale of data makes it hard for competitors to compete with. Marriott's expansion of its footprint across the globe made it a hospitality giant and hard to compete with.

In a December 2020 article for *Harvard Business Review* based on Jeff Bezo's book *Invent and Wander,* Bezos shares his thoughts on what is needed to play an infinite or "non-zero-sum" game: "Zero-sum games are unbelievably rare. Sporting events are zero-sum games. Two teams enter an arena. One's going to win; one's going to lose. Elections are zero-sum games. One candidate is going to win; one candidate is going to lose. In business, however, several competitors can do well. That's very normal. The most important thing for doing well against competition is to be both robust and nimble. And it is scale. Scale is a gigantic advantage because it gives you robustness. You can take a punch. But it's also good if you can dodge a punch. And that's the nimbleness. And as you get bigger, you grow more robust."

Bezos also shares the two critical factors for being nimble: your speed in making decisions and your ability to experiment. As you experiment, you will have failures, which is good because then you know what does not work, and you can kill the idea in its infancy. However, Bezos cautions us about two types of failure: First, experimental failure—that's the kind of failure you should be happy with. And then there's operational failure, which you should always try to prevent.

As Bezos states, "We've built hundreds of fulfillment centers at Amazon over the years, and we know how to do that. If we build a new fulfillment center and it's a disaster, that's just bad execution. That's not good failure." Blind arrogance is refusing to acknowledge, reflect on and avoid operational failure instead of celebrating it as an experimental failure.

Blind Arrogance	Empathetic Arrogance
Does not see a difference between operational failure and experimental failure	Accepts and learns from experimental failure but are hard and unaccepting of operational failure

KEY TAKEAWAYS

A clear mission or vision is a fundamental identity that gives an organization the much-needed foundation to build its competitive advantage to play an infinite game. And the best way to construct an advantage is by building a digital product with empathetic arrogance. Be empathetic with your customers; the more you listen to them, the clearer you will understand their problems. Frame the problem right. Be humble and continue to iterate with your customer until you get the right solution.

As you build digital products, explore features that enable you to grow your customer network. Think with a community mindset rather than creating a walled garden of features and data. Explore technology as a way to empower your customer. As you build, think scale while being nimble to change.

Blind Arrogance	Empathetic Arrogance
Think like mercenaries who want to build companies to flip	Think like missionaries who want to build companies to last
Creates a walled garden of data that provides the customer with a great personalized experience but refrains the customer from benefiting from others	Creates a community of data that gets richer as we sleep. Each customer's data contributes toward improving the experience for other customers
Does not see a difference between operational failure and experimental failure	Accepts and learns from experimental failure but are unyielding and unaccepting of operational failure

As the digital landscape continues to evolve, empathetic arrogance enables us to constantly learn and develop without losing the fundamental identity that

gives us a competitive advantage.

Conclusion

———

Equipped with an understanding of the ever-shifting digital landscape, we set out on a mission to build a digital product that is valuable to both the customer and the business. We are not mercenaries to the process. We are missionaries bound together by the company's vision and in love with the big, hairy, audacious problems ahead of us. We are ready to learn from and engage with every step of the process.

While confident in strengths and capabilities, we understand that we may not have the right solution or even be addressing the right problem. We move with empathy. Our passion may appear as arrogance as we are confident in our capabilities to learn and adapt while being empathetic with our customers. We are empathetically arrogant.

We show up at the table. We make room for our teammates. We lean on each other's skillsets. We trust each other. We are wholly tethered to the vision while being flexible within the solution.

We obsess about every little minute detail of our customers. We know there is a lot to learn about them that is not visible to the naked eye or shows up in our data. We listen and observe. We learn to identify the smallest detail that matters to our customers and offers them the most value. We collect the small emotional DNA our customers leave behind.

We make sure we, the team, are laser-focused on who our customer is. We define how we hold ourselves accountable to the customer. We align on the single view of the customer. We work backward and then forward. We identify vanity and clarity metrics that tell a complete story of the customer journey with our product.

We design with intent, with the customer. We have a complete, passionate, and empathetic understanding of what we are designing. We understand that the broader our understanding of the customer experience, the better design we will have. We also acknowledge that design is the functional element in a digital product that spurs action.

We use both small and big data to understand the customer and create products that humanizes the digital landscape for our customers. It is never about technology or us; it is always about the customer. In partnership with our technical partners, we build an agile product that can scale. We learn to create value faster instead of holding out for the perfect solution. We build in small increments, test it in the market and make changes based on customer feedback.

We learn to play the infinite game—delivering value to our customers while outlasting our competition. Our competitors are not necessarily in our industry. Our competitors are teams that have successfully grown their brand fans through their digital products. Our competitors help us identify gaps which are our growth opportunities. We learn and grow. We refuse to adapt and be stagnant. Because we know this is a digital war. Barriers to entry in the digital realm are low, even for an established product like ours that has a market monopoly. We are empathetically arrogant, and this enables us to evolve without losing the fundamental identity that gives us the competitive advantage.

Empathetic Arrogance

———

As I wrote this chapter, I toyed with the idea of including this as part of the conclusion. But I was concerned that some readers might see the table below as a checklist. I do want to emphasize this is **not** a checklist or a process to build digital products; this is the beginning of a new mindset and approach. Add to the table every time you catch yourself thinking of or doing something that falls under *blind arrogance*. Celebrate when you act with *empathetic arrogance*.

Lastly, may I ask you for a favor? If you read something in this book that sparked an idea in your head or changed the way you approach digital products, please share it with others. Share the book with your friends and colleagues and help me spread the word. Let us together humanize how we approach and build digital products. Let's empower our customers through our digital products so they consider the digital products to be an extension of themselves.

Thank you for reading, and happy building.

	Blind Arrogance	Empathetic Arrogance
Business model	We have a market monopoly and cannot be disrupted	Understand that barriers to entry in the digital realm are low, even for established platforms that have already captured a significant user base.
	Fixates on the same business model	Fixates on the changing customer behavior
	Defines business with technologies, offerings, or categories	Defines business with the problem solved for the customers
	Confident of business strengths and strategies	While confident in strengths and capabilities, understands that we may not have the right solution or even address the right problem
Mindset	Falls in love with the solution	Falls in love with the problem

Blind Arrogance	Empathetic Arrogance
Leads with technology to solve a problem	Leads with the customer to understand the problem
Adopts a mercenary mindset by following a process without questioning it	Adopts a missionary mindset by learning from and engaging with every step of the process
Holds out to the perfect solution for the big hairy problem	Provides customer value by identifying small critical problems that can ease the customer pain
Focuses on the short-term win	Focuses on playing small, interrelated games with vision on the long-term win. Each game or move helps move the company and the customer forward.

	Blind Arrogance	Empathetic Arrogance
	Every move must be a win, and the game ends.	Understands that we can sometimes be ahead and sometimes behind. The goal is the vision. To learn and improve and be better than yesterday, better than the last quarter, better than the last year. To continue to learn and grow or pivot, but continue to play
	Slow to change with the arrogance you have market monopoly	Continue to iterate on the product to surprise and delight the customer
Customer	Fixates on competition	Fixates on customer
	Every human is like all other humans	Every human is like some and maybe no other human

	Blind Arrogance	Empathetic Arrogance
	Assuming that a single digital product will work for everyone across the globe	Understands that user actions, as well as the social and political environment, impact digital products
	Confident in one's understanding of the customer's problem and the solution	Understands the customer asks but continues to validate and test the assumptions as the team builds
	Focuses on the customer in certain moments in time	Focuses on the customer in every interaction across the brand
Team	Leans on individual experience and wisdom	Leans on the collective wisdom of the team
	Selectively shares information across the team	Brings collective team to the table to discuss the business mission, customer needs, and product strategy

	Blind Arrogance	Empathetic Arrogance
Product	Confident in product features that improve business value	Explores product features that improve the customer experience while increasing business value
	What can I do to make this experience better?	What will it take for me to design an experience that makes you literally tell every single person you've ever encountered?
	Design is the "pretty" element in a digital product	Design is the functional element in a digital product that spurs action
	Design is secondary. We have a great technical solution.	The broader one's understanding of the human experience, the better product we will have.
	Designs for the customer	Designs with the customer

Blind Arrogance	Empathetic Arrogance
We are documenting requirements to share with our technical team. We are providing them with sufficient details so they know what to build	We have our technical team at the table with us discussing product strategy and how we can build a humanistic product that turns our customers into true brand fans
Does not see a difference between operational failure and experimental failure	Accepts and learns from experimental failure but is unyielding and unaccepting of operational failure
Thinks data is objective	Understands data is only as good as the data points we pull together to tell us the customer story
Leans on vanity metrics	Leans on clarity metrics to improve the product, thus increasing vanity metrics

Blind Arrogance	Empathetic Arrogance
Creates a walled garden of data that provides the customer with a great personalized experience but refrains the customer from benefiting from other users	Creates a community of data that gets richer as we sleep. Each customer's data contributes toward improving the experience for other customers
Focuses on data snapshots that highlight team or product performance	Focuses on event stream data that highlight the customer performance
Evaluates product performance data to identify new features	Engages with customers to understand their problems, blends them with data, and identifies new features

Blind Arrogance	Empathetic Arrogance
We will figure out the product marketing after we build the product.	Both product and marketing teams work collaboratively to understand the customer, the market, and the product. This ensures a holistic view of the product, the customer, and the complete customer journey.

Book Discussion Guide

———

The questions below have been provided by Beth Martin, a beta reader. After seeing my LinkedIn post asking for beta readers to review the manuscript, Beth offered to peruse it. She saw an opportunity to include book discussion topics and drafted these questions to enhance the reader's experience.

1. Consider **Part I** of this book and the author's goal to build a foundational mindset for digital products. Give examples of how the author does or does not achieve this. What are your takeaways?

2. The author describes her team, *Product Doomsday*, and how they led with blind arrogance. How might the team change the circumstances to operate in, or transition to, empathetic arrogance instead? (Chapter 1)

3. In Chapter 2, the author quotes Simon Sinek, who said: "The finite player is playing against its competitors; the infinite player is playing against themselves." In your own experience or citing examples from the book, compare and contrast the infinite player and the finite player. How

does this impact the infinite and finite players' distinct approaches?

4. The concept of Jobs To Be Done means that a customer "hires" a product to address an unmet need. How did SNHU understand what their customers value and need? Why would someone hire your product?

5. Consider **Part II** of this book. The author discusses obsession in the context of empathy. What does this mean for you? What are your takeaways?

6. In thinking about organizations that operate in blind arrogance and those that operate in empathetic arrogance, what characterizes those that could exist in the middle of the spectrum?

7. Inspired by Chapter 4, revisit a recent conversation from a personal or work context (or use another conversation described in the book elsewhere). Use the Think/Thoughts-Say/Said table format suggested by Professor Turner. What insights do you have about the opinions formed and how they affected your conversation? How might you more effectively reframe the conversation?

8. Why do you think 75 percent of Zappos' staff were willing to move? How does "customer obsession" translate for the employees? (Chapter 5)

9. Consider the case studies of the TripScout and Airbnb organizations and how they serve travelers. How could you reverse-engineer the best practices from those that

operate in empathetic arrogance to perform at "eleven stars"?

10. The author notes several "glocalization" examples, such as Starbucks in France. What are some lessons learned about how internationalization affects digital products?

11. In **Part III** of this book, the author explores four facets of digital products (marketing, design, technology, and data). Which is most important to you and why? Which is least important and why?

12. In Chapter 11, in the section Working Backward, the author describes a technique to write a press release to outline a successful digital product launch. What would you write about your current (or future ideal) digital product?

13. In **Part IV** of this book, digital Darwinism is connected to building a competitive advantage for digital products. How does this translate in our modern economy? How does this relate to your digital product?

14. "Digital product builders are change-makers" (Part II: Empathy). Do you agree or disagree? `What are some examples of this in practice?

15. What is the significance of the title? What title might you have given the book and why?

16. In the conclusion is a table summarizing the empathetic arrogance approaches. Which mindset speaks to you that you can immediately apply and why?

17. What should this book have covered but didn't?

Acknowledgments

—

As I started on my mission to humanize the digital landscape, I was unsure how the path would unfold and what unknowns awaited me. To increase my chance of success in writing my first book, I armed myself with a coach. I will forever be grateful to Eric Koester for his support and foresight.

Writing a book is an arduous task. I am indebted to my husband, who supported me every step of the way, including supporting my decision to quit my job to write. To my daughters, who encouraged me with their words, jokes, and cups of tea. At the onset, frustrated with my self-doubt, my eldest one said, "Stop crying and start writing." She did not realize the impact her words had on me. It became the war cry that helped me push through the dense fog.

My siblings, family, and friends, who never complained every time I said, "When the book is done...", and continued to cheer me on from the sidelines. I am thankful for your support. To my parents, who traveled from Canada and were with me during the final writing weeks. Thank you, mummy, for cooking and feeding me, allowing me to write while I juggled a new job. And, finally, to my dad, who kept reminding me to focus on the book and helping me finish strong.

It takes many iterations for a Minimum Viable Product (MVP) to be ready for final launch. Extremely grateful to these beta readers who gave up long hours to read, provide invaluable feedback on, and help shape this final product:

Beth Martin, Chui Chui Tan, Frances Dattilo, Gauri Shah, Hari Tagat, Katy Breuer, Michael Lewis, Michelle Saffir, Michelle Voorhies, Sanjay Kumar, Mike Hill

I am extremely grateful to Beth Martin, initially a stranger who offered to read my manuscript after seeing my LinkedIn post and has now helped shape the key elements by providing pointed feedback. She also saw the opportunity to include book discussion topics and drafted the questions that are included in this book. Beth, I am forever thankful to you for enhancing the reader experience.

A product need emerges from customer interviews. Detailed, in-depth, long conversations. This book, my product, was inspired by insightful interviews with these contributors:

Alex, Andy Asc, Chui Chui Tan, David Hogan, Jennifer Davis, James Nail, Jeanne Liu, Joel Rothstein, Ken Kellogg, Kyle Murdoch, Mark Rein, Mileha Suneji, Nancy Hersch, Nick, Owen Quinlan, Parag Tope, Santosh Subramanyam, Stephanie Slobodian, Ted Sodolka, Tim Streightiff

Just as a product needs customers, a book needs readers. Sincerely thankful to the early support of these readers for their confidence in me and my product—my first book:

Aashima Gupta, Adam Brock, Ajit Deshmukh, Amit Sharma, Ana Kalargyros, Andrea Bona, Andrew J. Fraser, Aneet Sahni, Anika Marpaka, Anurag Khaitan, Arvinder Goomer, Barbara Nivar, Bitsy Sawhney, Carolyn Semach, Celia DiNicola, Charles Ullan, Courtney Jorgensen, Daniel Kachura, Darshdeep Kaur Dhillon, Dave Austin, David Hogan, Debbie McDonald, Dhiraj Pardasani, Dinesh Bhaskaran, Divendra Sehgal, Elise Berkowitz, Elizabeth Phillips, Eric Koester, Fabiana Jenkins, Frances Dattilo, Giovanni Calabro, Girish Verma, George Corbin, Gulsheen Kaur, Gurpreet Anand, Harpreet K Groppe, Harpreet Sethi, Harpreet Singh, Harsharan Kaur, Howard Schwart, Indrani Som-Pandey, Indy Adenaw, Janet Wilson, Jason Ferrell, Jasprit Grover, Jasveen Kaur, Jasvinder Uberoi, Jaya Nessiar, Jayanthi Hariprasadh, Jeanne Liu, Jeffrey Goldfarb, Jeremy Wetzel, Jim Kelleher, John Punith, Joju Sebastian, Jonjie Sena, Joy Seo, Julia Evins, Julius Lai, Katie Wiggins, Katy Breuer, Kawaldeep Chadha, Kiran Kaur Kumar, Kristin Bartholomew, Kunwar Singh , Kyle Murdoch, Laurent Guinand, Laxmi Murthy, Lee Carson, Linda Crane , Lisa Martinez, Macon Morrison, Manish Baldua, Manjit Singh, Manmeet Broca, Manmohan Singh Sawhney, Marcia Rubain, Maria Rinaldi, Mary Beth DeLuzio, Mary G LoGiudice, Max Lang, Melissa Curtis, Michelle Cooper Neustadt, Michelle Haas, Michelle Henry, Michelle Saffir, Mike Hill, Miriam Prosnitz, Mohan Rao, Moses Merchant, Michael Lewis, Neerja Kathuria, Nikhil Kamdar, Ompriya Balamurugan, Pam Miller, Pam Nicholls, Lea Paradowski, Paramvir Soni, Pascale Brady, Preeti Batra,

Priya Sankaranarayanan, Rajashree Purohit, Rajeev Bhalla, Raminderjeet Kaur, Ravinder Birgi, Ravneet Sahni, Ripudaman Talwar, Rohit Anurag Satyasi, Romi K Sawhney, Rona Modanlo, Sandeep Singh, Santosh Subramanyam, Sarabjit Khanuja, Sarah Lukas, Saran Chhabra, Sheena Khurana, Simmi Singh, Simrin Saluja, Stacey Vance, Stephanie Slobodian, Suchi Dulloo, Suman Sharma, Swathi S Young, Tajinder Ahluwalia, Tanya Chakraborty, Tara Chait, Teresa O'Connor, Tharini Varadarajan, Tom Arundel, Tommie Adams, Troy Mitchell, Trusha M. Nikore, Tulsi Nandi, Ushma Agrawal, Vandana Chawla, Yogen Sanghani

Appendix

———

INTRODUCTION

Airbnb Newsroom. "About Us." Accessed on March 2, 2021. https://news.Airbnb.com/about-us/.

Anthony Scott, Viguerie Patrick, Schwartz Evan, Van Landeghem John. "2018 Corporate Longevity Forecast: Creative Destruction is Accelerating." February 2018. https://www.innosight.com/wp-content/uploads/2017/11/Innosight-Corporate-Longevity-2018.pdf.

Bank My Cell (blog). "How Many Smartphones are in the World?" Accessed on February 7, 2021. https://www.bankmycell.com/blog/how-many-phones-are-in-the-world.

Greylock. "Blitzscaling 18: Brian Chesky on Launching Airbnb and the Challenges of Scale." November 30, 2015. Video, 1:38:29. https://www.youtube.com/watch?v=W6o8u6sBFpo.

Merriam Webster Online, s.v. "Arrogance." Accessed on September 5, 2021. https://www.merriam-webster.com/dictionary/arrogance.

Solis, Brian. "Digital Darwinism and Why Brands die." *The Washington Post*, November 24, 2011. https://www.washingtonpost.com/national/on-innovations/digital-darwinism-and-why-brands-die/2011/11/20/gIQAR2jqlN_story.html.

Sun, Mengqi. "Businesses Predict Digital Transformation to Be Biggest Risk Factor in 2019." *The Wall Street Journal*, December 5, 2018. https://www.wsj.com/articles/businesses-predict-digital-transformation-to-be-biggest-risk-factor-in-2019-1544005926?tesla=y.

Tabrizi, Behnam, Ed Lam, Kirk Girard, and Vernon Irvin. "Digital Transformation Is Not About Technology." *Harvard Business Review*, March 31, 2019. https://hbr.org/2019/03/digital-transformation-is-not-about-technology.

Tocci, Meghan. "History and Evolution of Smartphones." Simple Texting (blog), accessed on January 15, 2021. https://simpletexting.com/where-have-we-come-since-the-first-smartphone/.

ZoBell, Steven. "Why Digital Transformations Fail: Closing The $900 Billion Hole In Enterprise Strategy." *Forbes*, March 13, 2018. https://www.forbes.com/sites/forbestechcouncil/2018/03/13/why-digital-transformations-fail-closing-the-900-billion-hole-in-enterprise-strategy/?sh=3670719c7b8b.

PART I

Scott, Anthony D., Viguerie Patrick, Schwartz Evan, Van Landeghem John. *2018 Corporate Longevity Forecast: Creative
Destruction is Accelerating. Boston.* February 2018. https://
www.innosight.com/wp-content/uploads/2017/11/Inno-
sight-Corporate-Longevity-2018.pdf

CHAPTER 1

Agrawal, Ravi. *India Connected: How the Smartphone is Transforming the World's Largest Democracy.* New York: Oxford
University Press, 2018.

Appolonia, Alexandra. "How BlackBerry went from controlling
the smartphone market to a phone of the past." *Business
Insider,* November 21, 2019. https://www.businessinsider.
com/blackberry-smartphone-rise-fall-mobile-failure-inno-
vate-2019-11.

Carey, Conner. "The Evolution of the iPhone: Every Model
from 2007–2020." *iPhone Life Magazine,* April 8, 2021.
https://www.iphonelife.com/content/evolution-iphone-ev-
ery-model-2007-2016.

Case, Amber. "We are all cyborgs now." Filmed December 2010
at TEDWomen2010, Washington, D.C. Video, 7:37. https://
www.ted.com/talks/amber_case_we_are_all_cyborgs_
now?language=en.

Christensen, Clayton, James Allworth, and Karen Dillon. *How
Will You Measure Your Life?.* New York: Harper Collins,
2012.

Devault, Gigi. "The History of Procter & Gamble's Brand Strategy." The Balance Small Business, August 20, 2019. https://www.thebalancesmb.com/market-research-history-brand-management-at-pandg-2297141.

Encyclopedia Britannica Online, s.v. "Cassette." Accessed on June 20, 2021. https://www.britannica.com/technology/cassette.

Encyclopedia Online. s.v. "Product Management." Accessed on June 21, 2021. https://www.encyclopedia.com/economics/encyclopedias-almanacs-transcripts-and-maps/product-management.

Eriksson, Martin. "What, exactly, is a Product Manager?" mind the PRODUCT, October 5, 2011. https://www.mindtheproduct.com/what-exactly-is-a-product-manager/.

Google LLC. "From the garage to the Googleplex." Accessed on June 25, 2021. https://about.google/our-story/.

Harvard Business School. "Clayton Christensen's "How Will You Measure Your Life?" Accessed on June 25, 2021. https://hbswk.hbs.edu/item/clayton-christensens-how-will-you-measure-your-life.

Harvard Business School. "Blockbuster: Its Failure and Lessons to Digital Transformers." Accessed on June 25, 2021. https://digital.hbs.edu/platform-digit/submission/blockbuster-its-failure-and-lessons-to-digital-transformers/#_ftn4.

Keelery, Sandhya. "Number of mobile phone internet users in India from 2015 to 2018 with a forecast until 2023." Mobile Internet & Apps. Statista. October 16, 2020. https://www.statista.com/statistics/558610/number-of-mobile-internet-user-in-india/.

Keelery, Sandhya. "Mobile phone internet user penetration in India from 2015 to 2018 with a forecast until 2023." Mobile Internet & Apps. Statista. February 2019. https://www.statista.com/statistics/309019/india-mobile-phone-internet-user-penetration/.

Knowledge@Wharton. "Why India's Smartphone Revolution Is a Double-edged Sword." January 22, 2019. https://knowledge.wharton.upenn.edu/article/indias-smartphone-revolution-double-edged-sword/.

McKinsey and Company. "The product management talent dilemma." November 28, 2018. https://www.mckinsey.com/industries/technology-media-and-telecommunications/our-insights/the-product-management-talent-dilemma.

National Geographic. "Y2K bug." Accessed on February 25, 2021. https://www.nationalgeographic.org/encyclopedia/Y2K-bug/.

Nielsen, Jakob. "A 100-Year View of User Experience." Nielsen Norman Group. December 24, 2017. https://www.nngroup.com/articles/100-years-ux/.

NN Group. "Don Norman: The term 'UX.'" July 2, 2016. Video, 1:49. https://www.youtube.com/watch?v=9BdtGjoIN4E.

Noguchi, Yuki. "Why Borders Failed While Barnes & Noble Survived." *NPR,* July 19, 2011. https://www.npr.org/2011/07/19/138514209/why-borders-failed-while-barnes-and-noble-survived.

NPR. "The Man Who Made You Put Away Your Pen." November 15, 2009. https://www.npr.org/templates/story/story.php?storyId=120364591.

NPR. "Ray Tomlinson, Inventor Of Modern Email, Dies." March 6, 2016. https://www.npr.org/2016/03/06/469428062/ray-tomlinson-inventor-of-modern-email-has-died.

Packard, David. *The HP Way: How Bill Hewlett and I Built Our Company.* New York City: Collins, 1995.

RankDex. "About RankDex." Accessed on June 25, 2021. http://www.rankdex.com/about.html.

World Wide Web. "W3 Project." Accessed on June 25, 2021. http://info.cern.ch/hypertext/WWW/TheProject.html.

CHAPTER 2

Apple. "The new iPod touch, Fun at full speed." Accessed June 21, 2021. https://www.apple.com/ipod-touch/.

Apple Newsroom. "New iPod touch delivers even greater performance." May 28, 2019. https://www.apple.com/newsroom/2019/05/new-ipod-touch-delivers-even-greater-performance/

Bass, Dina. "Microsoft Is Said to Stop Releasing New Models of the Zune." *Bloomberg*, March 14, 2011. https://www.bloomberg.com/news/articles/2011-03-14/microsoft-said-to-stop-releasing-new-zune-models-as-demand-ebbs.

Bishop, Todd. "Robbie Bach's four start-up lessons from Xbox and Zune." Geekwire. May 11, 2012. Accessed on December 22, 2020. https://www.geekwire.com/2012/robbie-bachs-lessons-intrapreneurship-xbox-zune/.

Cagan, Marty. "The Inconvenient Truth About Product." Silicon Valley Product Group. March 17, 2013. https://svpg.com/the-inconvenient-truth-about-product/.

Carse, James. *Finite and Infinite Games*. New York: The Free Press, 1986.

Clark, Liat. "Waze cofounder: 'fall in love with the problem, not the solution'." *WIRED*, October 20, 2014. https://www.wired.co.uk/article/waze-uri-levine.

Conley, Randy. "Simon Sinek's 5 Steps for Mastering the "Infinite" Game of Leadership." Blanchard LeaderChat. October 27, 2017. https://leaderchat.org/2017/10/27/simon-sineks-5-steps-for-mastering-the-infinite-game-of-leadership/.

Esser, Joerg. "The Secret of Adaptable Organizations Is Trust." *Harvard Business Review*, March 15, 2021. https://hbr.org/2021/03/the-secret-of-adaptable-organizations-is-trust?ab=hero-main-text.

Ganapati, Priya. "GameStop to Stop Zune Sales." *theStreet*, May 23, 2008. https://www.thestreet.com/technology/gamestop-to-stop-zune-sales-10418052.

Lencioni, Patrick. *The Five Dysfunctions of a Team: A Leadership Fable*. San Francisco: Jossey-Bass, 2011.

Parkinson's Foundation. "Statistics." Accessed on June 20, 2021. https://www.parkinson.org/Understanding-Parkinsons/Statistics.

Russell Ackoff, Daniel Greenberg. *Turning Learning Right Side Up: Putting Education Back on Track*. New Jersey: Prentice Hall, 2008.

Sinek, Simon. *The Infinite Game*. London: Portfolio, 2019.

Start With Why (blog). "Blow Up Your Business Before Someone Else Does." November 2011. https://blog.startwithwhy.com/refocus/2011/10/blow-up-your-business-before-someone-else-does.html.

Suneji, Mileha. "Simple Hacks for Life with Parkinson's." Filmed February 2015 at *TEDxDelft*, *6:48*. https://www.ted.com/talks/mileha_soneji_simple_hacks_for_life_with_parkinson_s?language=en.

United States Securities and Exchange Commission. "For the fiscal year ended September 24, 2016." Accessed on March 30, 2021. https://www.sec.gov/Archives/edgar/data/320193/000162828016020309/a201610-k9242016.htm.

CHAPTER 3

Adams, Susan. "Meet the English Professor Creating The Billion-Dollar College Of The Future." Forbes. March 28, 2019. https://www.forbes.com/sites/susanadams/2019/03/28/meet-the-english-professor-creating-the-billion-dollar-college-of-the-future/?sh=191bdafe426b.

Anthony, Scott. "Kodak's Downfall Wasn't About Technology" *Harvard Business Review*, July 15, 2016. https://hbr.org/2019/03/digital-transformation-is-not-about-technology.

Bandler, James. "Kodak Signs Agreement to Buy Online Photo Company Ofoto." *The Wall Street Journal*, May 1, 2001. https://www.wsj.com/articles/SB988662149797022094.

Bloomberg Business. "Steve Jobs: `There's Sanity Returning." March 25, 1998. https://www.bloomberg.com/news/articles/1998-05-25/steve-jobs-theres-sanity-returning.

Christensen, Clayton M., Taddy Hall, Karen Dillon, David S. Duncan. "Know Your Customers' "Jobs to Be Done." *Harvard Business Review*, September 2016. https://hbr.org/2016/09/know-your-customers-jobs-to-be-done.

Christensen, Clayton M., Scott Cook and Taddy Hall. "What Customers Want from Your Products." Harvard Business School. January 16, 2006. https://hbswk.hbs.edu/item/what-customers-want-from-your-products.

Cohan, Peter. "How Success Killed Eastman Kodak." *Forbes*, October 1, 2011. https://www.forbes.com/sites/petercohan/2011/10/01/how-success-killed-eastman-kodak/?sh=4a-c5e4ea637a.

Drucker, Peter. *The Five Most Important Questions You Will Ever Ask About Your Organization*. San Francisco: Jossey-Bass, 1993.

Economy, Peter. "5 Essential Questions for Entrepreneurs" *Inc*, September 5, 2013. https://www.inc.com/peter-economy/5-essential-questions-entrepreneurs.html.

EHL Insights. "Meet the biggest hotel chains in the world." Accessed on March 20, 2021. https://hospitalityinsights.ehl.edu/biggest-hotel-chains.

Marriott. "Investor Relations." Accessed on March 8, 2021. https://marriott.gcs-web.com/investor-faqs.

Reinhardt, Andy. "There's Sanity Returning." The Business-Week, May 25, 1998. *https://www.bloomberg.com/news/articles/1998-05-25/steve-jobs-theres-sanity-returning.*

Solis, Brian. "The New Kodak Moment = That Moment When You Lose Market Relevance." *Brian Solas* (blog), June 14, 2017. https://www.briansolis.com/2017/06/new-kodak-moment-moment-lose-market-relevance/.

Vlaskovits, Patrick. "Henry Ford, Innovation, and That "Faster Horse" Quote." *Harvard Business Review,* August 20, 2011. https://hbr.org/2011/08/henry-ford-never-said-the-fast.

Wedell-Wedellsborg, Thomas. "Are You Solving the Right Problems?" *Harvard Business Review*, January–February 2017. https://hbr.org/2017/01/are-you-solving-the-right-problems.

Willy, Shih. "The Real Lessons From Kodak's Decline." MIT SLOAN, March 20, 2016. https://secure.dashdigital.com/mitsmr/summer_2016?article_id=1107485&pg=NaN#pgNaN.

CHAPTER 4

Calder, Simon. "Michael O' Leary Launches Ryanair's 'Always Getting Better' plan." *Independent*, March 26, 2014. https://www.independent.co.uk/travel/news-and-advice/michael-o-leary-launches-ryanair-s-always-getting-better-plan-9217455.html.

Grant, Adam. *Think Again: The Power of Knowing What You Don't Know*. New York: Viking, 2021.

Inc. Staff. "How Spanx Got Started." *Inc.*, June 17, 2021. https://www.inc.com/sara-blakely/how-sara-blakley-started-spanx.html.

Klar, Rebecca. "House Democrats use Markup app for leadership contest voting." *The Hill*, December 4, 2020. https://thehill.com/policy/technology/528752-house-democrats-use-markup-app-for-leadership-contest-voting.

Merriam Webster Online, s.v. "Empathy." Accessed on April 5, 2021. https://www.merriam-webster.com/dictionary/empathy.

Markup Labs. "Products." Accessed on March 5, 2021. https://www.markuplabs.com/products.

Markup Labs. "Statement: Markup ERVS App Used by House Dems for First Remote Votes by US Congress." Dec 8, 2020. https://www.markuplabs.com/post/markup-ervs-remote-voting-app-used-by-house-dems-for-first-remote-votes-in-us-congress.

The Editorial Board. "Washington Post: Skeptical that Congress can vote Remotely? It's already happening." *The Washington Post,* Dec 13, 2020. https://www.washingtonpost.com/opinions/skeptical-that-congress-can-vote-remotely-its-already-happening/2020/12/11/465819ec-3665-11eb-8d38-6aea1adb3839_story.html

CHAPTER 5

Amazon Staff. "Our Mission." Amazon. Accessed on June 15, 2021. https://www.aboutamazon.co.uk/uk-investment/our-mission.

Bain & Company. "Are you experienced?" Infographic. April 08, 2015. https://www.bain.com/insights/are-you-experienced-infographic/.

Chesky, Brian."HANDCRAFTED." May 3, 2017. In *Masters of Scale.* Produced by Reid Hoffman. Podcast, MP3 audio. 29:00. https://mastersofscale.com/brian-chesky-handcrafted/.

Debruyne, Frédéric and Andreas Dullweber. "The Five Disciplines of Customer Experience Leaders." Brief. Bain &

Company. April 08, 2015. https://www.bain.com/insights/
the-five-disciplines-of-customer-experience-leaders/#.

Greylock. "Blitzscaling 18: Brian Chesky on Launching Airbnb
and the Challenges of Scale." November 30, 2015. Video,
1:38:29. https://www.youtube.com/watch?v=W608u6sBFp0.

Hsieh, Tony. "CEO Letter: 'Zappos And Amazon Sitting In A
Tree." Zappos.com. July 22, 2009. https://www.zappos.com/
about/stories/zappos-and-amazon.

Hsieh, Tony. "Zappos' CEO on Using Corporate Reloca-
tion to Preserve Customer-Led Culture." *Harvard Business Review,* January 3, 2014. https://hbr.org/2014/01/
zappos-ceo-on-using-corporate-relocation-to-pre-
serve-customer-led-culture.

Kirby, Julia and Thomas A. Stewart. "The Institutional Yes."
Harvard Business Review, October 2007. https://hbr.
org/2007/10/the-institutional-yes.

Lexicon online. s.v. "Obsession." Accessed on April 10, 2021.
https://www.lexico.com/definition/Obsession.

Sabanoglu, Tugba. "Projected retail e-commerce GMV share
of Amazon in the United States from 2016 to 2021." B2C
E-Commerce. Statistica. December 1, 2020. https://www.
statista.com/statistics/788109/amazon-retail-market-share-
usa/.

Warren, Roxanne. "10 Things To Know About Zappos Customer Service." About. Zappos. April 17th, 2020. https://www.zappos.com/about/stories/customer-service-things-to-know.

07272009july. "Video from Jeff Bezos about Amazon and Zappos." July 22, 2009. Video, 8:09. https://www.youtube.com/watch/-hxX_Q5CnaA.

CHAPTER 6

App Store Preview. "TikTok." Apple. Accessed May 12, 2019. https://apps.apple.com/us/app/tiktok/id835599320.

Britt, Phil. "How Can Brands Balance Human vs. Digital Experiences?." *CMS Wire*, February 1, 2021. https://www.cmswire.com/customer-experience/how-can-brands-balance-human-vs-digital-experiences/.

Chan, Connie. "When AI is the Product: The Rise of AI-Based Consumer Apps." Andreessen Horowitz. December 3, 2018. https://a16z.com/2018/12/03/when-ai-is-the-product-the-rise-of-ai-based-consumer-apps/.

Encyclopaedia Britannica Online. s.v. "Glocalization." Accessed June 15, 2021. https://www.britannica.com/topic/glocalization.

Fannin, Rebecca. "The Strategy Behind TikTok's Global Rise." *Harvard Business Review*, September 13, 2019. https://hbr.org/2019/09/the-strategy-behind-tiktoks-global-rise.

Hayes, Adam. "Glocalization." *Investopedia*, March 26, 2020.
https://www.investopedia.com/terms/g/glocalization.asp.

Immelt, Jeffrey R., Govindarajan Vijay, Trimble Chris."How GE
Is Disrupting Itself." *Harvard Business Review*, October 2009.
https://hbr.org/2009/10/how-ge-is-disrupting-itself?auto-
complete=true.

Laurent, Lionel. "Starbucks adapts to Gallic tastes in growth
quest." Reuters, May 27, 2010. https://www.reuters.com/arti-
cle/us-starbucks-france-idCATRE64Q3LW20100527.

Li, Feng. "Why Western Digital Firms Have Failed in China."
Harvard Business Review, August 14, 2018. https://hbr.
org/2018/08/why-western-digital-firms-have-failed-in-china.

Rocco. "Tiktok and Douyin are not the same." March 27, 2019.
https://chinasocialmedia.net/tiktok-and-douyin-are-not-
the-same/.

Sherman, Alex. "TikTok reveals detailed user numbers for
the first time." *CNBC*, August 24, 2020. https://www.cnbc.
com/2020/08/24/tiktok-reveals-us-global-user-growth-num-
bers-for-first-time.html.

Sherwin, Katie. "Cultural Nuances Impact User Experience:
Why We Test with International Audiences." Nielsen Norman Group. June 26, 2016. https://www.nngroup.com/arti-
cles/cultural-nuances/.

CHAPTER 7

Bariso, Justin. "Amazon Has a Secret Weapon Known as "Working Backwards"—and It Will Transform the Way You Work." *Inc.*, December 16, 2019. https://www.inc.com/justin-bariso/amazon-uses-a-secret-process-for-launching-new-ideas-and-it-can-transform-way-you-work.html.

Dallke, Jim. "Tripscout raises $2.3M as travel industry prepares for a comeback." *BizJournals Chicago Inno*, March 16, 2021. https://www.bizjournals.com/chicago/inno/stories/fundings/2021/03/16/tripscout-raises.html.

Experian Information Technology, Beijing. "How to achieve the single customer view." White Paper. Accessed on March 10, 2021. https://www.experian.com.cn/wp-content/uploads/2018/10/Single-Customer-View-CN-.pdf

Live Better With. "Main Page." Assessed May 16, 2021. https://livebetterwith.com/.

Lubowicka, Karolina and Karolina Matuszewska. "Single customer view (SCV): what is it and how does it work?" *Piwik Pro* (blog), July 30, 2019. https://piwik.pro/blog/what-is-single-customer-view-and-how-does-it-work/.

Maruya, Ash. "Why Lean Canvas vs Business Model Canvas?" *Leanstack* (blog), February 27, 2012. https://blog.leanstack.com/why-lean-canvas-vs-business-model-canvas/.

McAllister, Ian, "What is Amazon's approach to product development and product management?" May 18, 2012. https://

www.quora.com/What-is-Amazons-approach-to-product-development-and-product-management?ref=http://www.product-frameworks.com/.

Rawson, Alexis, Ewan Duncan, and Conor Jones. "The Truth About Customer Experience." *Harvard Business Review*, September 2013. https://hbr.org/2013/09/the-truth-about-customer-experience.

Sweetwood, Adele. "How One Company Used Data to Rethink the Customer Journey." *Harvard Business Review*, August 23, 2016. https://hbr.org/2016/08/how-one-company-used-data-to-rethink-the-customer-journey.

CHAPTER 8

App Store. "Waze Navigation & Live Traffic." Accessed on June 26, 2021. https://apps.apple.com/us/app/waze-navigation-live-traffic/id323229106.

Benartzi, Shlomo and Saurabh Bhargava. "How Digital Design Drives User Behavior." *Harvard Business Review*, February 3, 2020. https://hbr.org/2020/02/how-digital-design-drives-user-behavior.

Google Play Store. "Waze - GPS, Maps, Traffic Alerts & Live Navigation." Accessed on June 26, 2021. https://play.google.com/store/apps/details?id=com.waze&hl=en_US&gl=US.

Naomi Staff. "Research: Humanising Data." Core Research. Assessed on January 25, 2021. https://onecore.ie/intel/outlook/humanising-data/.

Pentagram. "Waze Brand Identity." Accessed on Jan 30, 2021. https://www.pentagram.com/work/waze/story.

Sheppard, Benedict, Sarrazin Hugo, Kouyoumjian Garen, and Dore Fabricio. "The business value of design." McKinsey & Company. October 25, 2018. https://www.mckinsey.com/business-functions/mckinsey-design/our-insights/the-business-value-of-design.

Vashishtha, Yashica. "Waze : The Israeli Build, Play, Monetize Mapping App that Acquired the Attention of Google." *Your Tech Story*, November 2, 2019. https://www.yourtechstory.com/2019/11/02/waze-israeli-build-play-monetize-mapping-app-acquired-attention-google/.

Waze. "Under the Hood: Behind the Brand Refresh." *Medium* (blog), June 29, 2020. https://medium.com/waze/under-the-hood-behind-the-brand-refresh-95a4c23e42e.

Waze. "Driving Change with Hila, Head of Communities at Waze." *Medium* (blog), November 9, 2020. https://medium.com/waze/driving-change-with-hila-head-of-communities-at-waze-2d9fe1bb78d2.

Wolf, Gary. "Steve Jobs: The Next Insanely Great Thing." *Wired*, February 1, 1996. https://www.wired.com/1996/02/jobs-2/.

CHAPTER 9

Agile Manifesto. "Manifesto for Agile Software Development." Accessed on June 15, 2021. https://agilemanifesto.org/.

Ittycheria, Pradeep. "Don't Hide The Business Strategy From Your Technology Teams." *Forbes*, September 24, 2019. https://www.forbes.com/sites/forbestechcouncil/2019/09/24/dont-hide-the-business-strategy-from-your-technology-teams/?sh=7a028a2e465f.

Knowledge@Wharton. "Mercenaries vs. Missionaries: John Doerr Sees Two Kinds of Internet Entrepreneurs." UPenn. April 13, 2020. https://knowledge.wharton.upenn.edu/article/mercenaries-vs-missionaries-john-doerr-sees-two-kinds-of-internet-entrepreneurs/.

Krieger, Colleen. "Becoming a Bot: How Capital One's AI Design Team Created the Character Eno." Capital One. September 29, 2017. https://www.capitalone.com/tech/machine-learning/becoming-a-bot-how-capital-ones-ai-design-team-created-the-character-eno/.

Latif, Maria, Toseef Aslam, Palwashay Sehar. "Impact of domain knowledge in phase of requirement engineering." Research Gate, November 2018. https://www.researchgate.net/publication/335777274_Impact_of_domain_knowledge_in_phase_of_requirement_engineering.

Mayer, Margaret. "How and Why We Built Eno's NLP In-House." Capital One. September 26, 2018. https://www.capitalone.com/tech/machine-learning/capital-ones-intelligent-assistant-why-we-built-enos-nlp-tech-in-house/.

CHAPTER 10

Audioburst. "How Small Data Made Lego The Largest Toy Company In The World." September 6, 2016. Video, 3:06. https://www.youtube.com/watch?v=MLuN98kzAvc.

First Round Review. "I'm Sorry, But Those Are Vanity Metrics." Accessed February 22, 2021. https://review.firstround.com/im-sorry-but-those-are-vanity-metrics.

Knowledge@Wharton. "Why Small Data Is the New Big Data." March 24, 2016. https://knowledge.wharton.upenn.edu/article/small-data-new-big-data/.

Lindstorm, Martin. *Small Data: The Tiny Clues That Uncover Huge Trends.* New York: St. Martins Press, 2016.

Lupi, Giorgia, Stefanie Posavec, and Maria Popova. *Dear Data.* New York: Princeton Architectural Press, 2016.

Pentagram. "Waze Brand Identity." Accessed on Jan 30, 2021. https://www.pentagram.com/work/waze/story.

Poptech. "Data is about people." November 7, 2015. Video, 14:41. https://www.youtube.com/watch?v=SbqNEKygFiA.

Randy Bean, Thomas H. Davenport. "Companies Are Failing in Their Efforts to Become Data-Driven." *Harvard Business Review*, February 5, 2019. https://hbr.org/2019/02/companies-are-failing-in-their-efforts-to-become-data-driven.

Robertson, David and Bill Breen. *Brick by Brick: How LEGO Rewrote the Rules of Innovation and Conquered the Global Toy Industry.* New York: Crown Business, 2014.

Wahbe, Andrea. "How To Maintain A Personal Touch With Customers As You Grow." ShopifyPlus. September 28, 2015. https://www.shopify.com/enterprise/63971715-how-to-maintain-a-personal-touch-with-customers-as-you-grow.

Waze. *Connected Citizens Program.* Accessed May 22, 2021. https://web-assets.waze.com/partners/ccp/WAZE-CCP-Factsheet.pdf.

Waze. "Driving Change with Hila, Head of Communities at Waze." *Medium.com* (blog), November 9, 2020. https://medium.com/waze/driving-change-with-hila-head-of-communities-at-waze-2d9fe1bb78d2.

Waze. "Driving Change with Hila, Head of Communities at Waze." *Medium.com* (blog), https://wazeopedia.waze.com/wiki/USA/Main_Page/Drive_with_Waze_on.

Waze. "Under the Hood: Behind the Brand Refresh." *Medium.com* (blog), June 29, 2020. https://medium.com/waze/under-the-hood-behind-the-brand-refresh-95a4c23e42e.

Wazopedia. "Just drive around with Waze turned on." Waze. Accessed June 20, 2021. https://wazeopedia.waze.com/wiki/Global/Just_drive_around_with_Waze_turned_on.

CHAPTER 11

Beales, Richard. "Breakingviews - Direct listings will move nearer IPOs – and Europe." *Reuters*, April 1, 2018. https://cn.reuters.com/article/us-usa-ipos-breakingviews-idUSKBN1YV1FF.

Bezos, Jeff. "How Amazon Thinks About Competition." *Harvard Business Review*, December 21, 2020. https://hbr.org/2020/12/how-amazon-thinks-about-competition.

Bezos, Jeff and Walter Isaacson. *Invent and Wander: The Collected Writings of Jeff Bezos. Boston: Harvard Business Review and PublicAffairs,* 2021.

Cowan, Matt. "Inside the clone factory: the story of the Samwer brothers and Rocket Internet." *Wired*, February 3, 2012. https://www.wired.co.uk/article/inside-the-clone-factory.

Currier, James. "What Makes Data Valuable: The Truth About Data Network Effects." NFX. Accessed on December 20, 2021. https://www.nfx.com/post/truth-about-data-network-effects/.

Furrier, John. "Exclusive: The Story of AWS and Andy Jassy's Trillion Dollar Baby." *Medium.com* (blog), January 29. 2015. https://medium.com/@furrier/original-content-the-story-of-aws-and-andy-jassys-trillion-dollar-baby-4e8a35f-d7ed.

Greylock. "Blitzscaling 18: Brian Chesky on Launching Airbnb and the Challenges of Scale." November 30, 2015. Video, 1:38:29. https://www.youtube.com/watch?v=W6o8u6sBFpo.

Hagiu, Andrei and Julian Wright. "When Data Creates Competitive Advantage." *Harvard Business Review*, January–February 2020. https://hbr.org/2020/01/when-data-creates-competitive-advantage.

Insights Team. "How Pandora knows what you want to hear next?" Forbes. October 1, 2019. https://www.forbes.com/sites/insights-teradata/2019/10/01/how-pandora-knows-what-you-want-to-hear-next/?sh=613785e73902.

Issacson, Walter. *Invent and Wander: The Collected Writings of Jeff Bezos.* Boston: Harvard Business Review Press and PublicAffairs, 2020.

Jelčić, Dora. "Wimbdu - A Story of Airbnb's Clone." *Playing Lean* (blog), August 31,2020. https://www.playinglean.com/blogs/playing-lean-blog/wimdu-a-story-of-Airbnbs-clone.

Lidsky, David. "The definitive timeline of Spotify's critic-defying journey to rule music." *Fast Company*, August 6, 2018. https://www.fastcompany.com/90205527/the-definitive-timeline-of-spotifys-critic-defying-journey-to-rule-music.

Pandora. "About The Music Genome Project®." Accessed on January 30, 2021. https://www.pandora.com/about/mgp.

Pandora. "Pandora Account Privacy FAQ." Help. Accessed on Jan 23, 2021. https://help.pandora.com/s/article/Information-about-Privacy-on-Pandora-1519949298664?language=en_US#zc.

Richter, Felix. "Amazon Leads $130-Billion Cloud Market." Infrastructure as a Service (IaaS). Statistica. February 4, 2021. https://www.statista.com/chart/18819/worldwide-market-share-of-leading-cloud-infrastructure-service-providers/.

Sanghvi, Vir. "Why Marriott is number one..." *Hindustan Times,* April 28, 2018. https://www.hindustantimes.com/brunch/why-marriott-is-number-one/story-aa40JwQYdCG-Zdtck3waHAM.html.

Sharma, Asit. "4 Competitive Advantages Marriott International Wants Shareholders to Grasp." *Motley Fool,* September 13, 2018. https://www.fool.com/investing/2018/09/13/4-competitive-advantages-marriott-international-wa.aspx.

Synergy Research. "Cloud Market Ends 2020 on a High while Microsoft Continues to Gain Ground on Amazon." February 2, 2021. https://www.srgresearch.com/articles/cloud-market-ends-2020-high-while-microsoft-continues-gain-ground-amazon.

Tsotsis, Alexia. "Airbnb Freaks Out Over Samwer Clones." *Techcrunch,* June 9, 2011. https://techcrunch.com/2011/06/09/Airbnb/.

Waniata, Ryan and Quentyn Kennemer. "Spotify vs. Pandora." Digital Trends. February 7, 2021. https://www.digitaltrends.com/music/spotify-vs-pandora/.